MEDIEVAL FINANCE

MEDIEVAL FINANCE

A COMPARISON OF FINANCIAL INSTITUTIONS

IN NORTHWESTERN EUROPE

BRYCE LYON AND A. E. VERHULST

BROWN UNIVERSITY PRESS

PROVIDENCE, RHODE ISLAND

1967

This is the 143rd volume in a series of works sponsored by the Faculty of Letters of the University of Ghent. It is distributed in Continental Europe and Great Britain by De Tempel, 37 Tempelhof, Bruges, Belgium.

Library of Congress Catalogue Card Number: 67-19657

Second Printing, 1968

Printed in the United States of America

CONTENTS

Chapter I

INTRODUCTION

In the history of the western world there has probably been no period when historians have seen more unity of spirit, culture, and institutions than during the Middle Ages. The very words "Western Christendom" symbolize a time when western Europe was united by a common Christian faith. Historians writing about the church in the Middle Ages speak of developments peculiar to Germany, France, and England, but within the framework of the "medieval church." The eleventh-century reform of the church, the Crusades, monasticism, and the papacy were phenomena embracing all western Europe. When historians concentrate upon particular manifestations of these phenomena they do so with a realization that they were but parts of European movements. The Cistercians in England were but doing what their brothers were doing in France, Italy, or the Low Countries. One canon law and theology served the numerous political units of Europe. So it was with the other typical manifestations of medieval civilization. There was Romanesque and Gothic architecture, the university, Latin and vernacular literature. Historians recognize a seignorial system gripping all western Europe, a feudal system by which men fought and governed, an economic birth which revitalized western Europe, the medieval town with its bourgeoisie, and the new social and economic forces created by the increased circulation of money. However much medievalists may delight in uncovering variations, most have emphasized the unity of the Middle Ages. And those, like H. Pirenne, M. Bloch, H. O. Taylor, E. Gilson, and K. Lamprecht, who have skillfully described and interpreted manifestations of this unity are regarded as first among their peers[1].

[1] See, for example, H. Pirenne, *Les villes du moyen âge: Essai d'histoire*

But how different has been the approach of the historian when writing on medieval institutions. Here nationalism, chauvinism, and particularism rise to impose themselves as barriers. Despite the expression "medieval institutions," when governmental institutions are investigated they invariably become English, German, French, Italian, Flemish, and Spanish. Few historians have studied medieval government in the fashion that has been applied to other ingredients of medieval civilization[1]. There have been exceptions with medieval law and kingship and, more recently, with representative and parliamentary institutions, but even here few have been the attempts to discuss these institutions in the comparative fashion that has characterized study of the town, feudalism, and seignorialism[2].

To understand the psychological and emotional reasons for the lack of comparative study of medieval institutions is not to lessen the regret that such study has been neglected, especially in view of the fact that research on the institutional development of medieval states has a longer tradition and a greater intensity than exists on other aspects of the Middle Ages. Legion are the fine scholars who have devoted themselves to the institutions of their countries. Among those who have provided great syntheses are W. Stubbs, F. W. Maitland, and T. F. Tout of England; P. Viollet, A. Luchaire, and R. Fawtier of France;

économique et sociale (Brussels, 1927), Histoire économique et sociale du moyen âge (édition revue et mise à jour avec une annexe bibliographie et critique by H. Van Werveke, Paris, 1963). These works appeared in English in 1925 and 1937 respectively. See also M. Bloch, La société féodale (Paris, 1939-1940), vols. I-II, which appeared in English as Feudal Society (London, 1961); H. O. Taylor, The Mediaeval Mind: A History of the Development of Thought and Emotion in the Middle Ages (4th ed., London, 1925), vols. I-II; E. Gilson, The Spirit of Medieval Philosophy (New York, 1936); K. Lamprecht, Deutsches Wirtschaftsleben im Mittelalter (Leipzig, 1886), vols. I-IV.

[1] An exception to this statement is, of course, H. Mitteis, Der Staat des Hohen Mittelalters (4th ed., Weimar, 1953).

[2] For example, F. Kern, Kingship and the Law in the Middle Ages (Oxford, 1939); P. E. Schramm, Der König von Frankreich; das Wesen der Monarchie vom 9. zum 16. Jahrhundert (2d ed., Weimar, 1960), and A History of the English Coronation (Oxford, 1937). See also Schramm's studies on German kingship. See the Studies Presented to the International Commission for the History of Representative and Parliamentary Institutions, especially the remarks of B. Lyon in vol. XXIV, "Medieval Constitutionalism: a Balance of Power," in Album Helen Maud Cam (Louvain, 1961), pp. 157-183.

8

and G. Waitz, J. Ficker, and H. Mitteis of Germany[1]. From their works plus the shorter studies and fine editions of pertinent records made available during the present century our knowledge of what may be described as "national institutions" during the Middle Ages is unusually complete. Beyond this point, however, little has been done. Except for a few haphazard attempts to compare the institutional development of medieval states and except for generalizations such as that the institutional development of France lagged behind that of England by a hundred years, there have been no scholarly efforts to ascertain the similarities and diversities of central and local institutions in the principal states of medieval Europe[2].

Where this local spirit is particularly evident and where it should be less so because of the richer documentation is with financial institutions. In that part of western Europe bound so tightly together by political and economic ties—the Île de France, Normandy, Flanders, and England—there has been no comparative study of financial institutions except for the English and Norman systems of finance. Despite the superiority of the earlier and richer English documentation the other regions are not without their records which could throw light on such questions as the following. Beyond the Norman exchequer did the English exchequer and its system of administration have counterparts

[1] W. Stubbs, *The Constitutional History of England* (Oxford, 1874-1878), vols. I-III; F. Pollock and F. W. Maitland, *The History of English Law Before the Time of Edward I* (2d ed., Cambridge, 1895), vols. I-II; T. F. Tout, *Chapters in the Administrative History of Mediaeval England* (Manchester, 1920-1933), vols. I-VI; P. Viollet, *Histoire des institutions politiques et administratives de la France* (Paris, 1890-1903), vols. I-III; A. Luchaire, *Histoire des institutions monarchiques de la France sous les premiers Capétiens (987-1180)* (2d ed., Paris, 1891), vols. I-II; R. Fawtier, *Les Capétiens et la France* (Paris, 1942), which appeared in English as *The Capetian Kings of France* (London, 1960); G. Waitz, *Deutsche Verfassungsgeschichte* (Kiel, 1874-1885), vols. I-VIII; J. Ficker, *Untersuchungen zur Rechtsgeschichte* (Innsbruck, 1891-1904), vols. I-VI.

[2] For example, Ch. Petit-Dutaillis, *La monarchie féodale en France et en Angleterre, Xe-XIIIe siècle* (Paris, 1933), which appeared in English as *The Feudal Monarchy in France and England* (London, 1936); R. Fawtier, *L'Europe Occidentale de 1270 à 1328*, in *Histoire du moyen âge* (Paris, 1940), vol. VI; J. R. Strayer and C. H. Taylor, *Studies in Early French Taxation* (Cambridge, Mass., 1939). There are also certain comparisons in F. Lot and R. Fawtier, *Histoire des institutions françaises au moyen âge* (Paris, 1957-1958), vols. I-II.

elsewhere on the Continent? Was the English exchequer and its system the first to develop and was it better developed than other systems? What were the institutional influences which spilled back and forth? Did the English system influence other systems and vice versa? What were the principal revenues and expenses of these states and how did they vary? How did the systems of record-keeping compare? Did these financial institutions develop apart from any outside influence and solely in response to demands common to western Europe? How did these financial institutions reflect the tempo of political, economic, and social development?

These questions, fundamental to our understanding of European institutional development, need to be answered but have thus far been ignored except in the studies of T. Stapleton and F. M. Powicke devoted to the Norman and English exchequers and the more general works of C. H. Haskins, H. Pirenne, and F. L. Ganshof[1]. The recent publication in Belgium, however, of an extremely important financial record has given hope of answering some of these questions, at least for the twelfth century. Following his fortunate discovery of a manuscript at Metz in 1958, M. Gysseling collaborated with A. E. Verhulst in a definitive edition of the principal general financial account of Flanders for 1187—the so-called *Grote Brief*. Verhulst and Gysseling made a few comparisons of Flemish financial institutions with those of Normandy and England but in such a general vein that they but underscored some of the observations of Haskins[2]. Appreciating the fine opportunity presented by the *Grote Brief*, Verhulst and Lyon decided, therefore, to collaborate further in a brief comparative study of the Flemish, Capetian, Norman, and English institutions during the twelfth century.

[1] T. Stapleton, *Magni Rotuli Scaccarii Normanniae sub Regibus Angliae* (London, 1840-1844), vols. I-II; F. M. Powicke, *The Loss of Normandy, 1189-1204* (2d ed., Manchester, 1961); C. H. Haskins, *Norman Institutions* (Cambridge, Mass., 1918); H. Pirenne, *Histoire de Belgique* (5th ed., Brussels, 1929), vol. I; F. L. Ganshof, "La Flandre," in Lot and Fawtier, *Institutions françaises*, I, 343-426. See also J. Boussard, "Les institutions financières de l'Angleterre au xiie siècle," *Cahiers de Civilisation Médiévale*, I (1958).

[2] A. Verhulst and M. Gysseling, *Le Compte Général de 1187, connu sous le nom de "Gros Brief," et les institutions financières du comté de Flandre au XIIe siècle* (Brussels, 1962), pp. 9-26.

Of the chapters that follow Verhulst has written those dealing with Flemish financial institutions and the comparison of the Flemish, Capetian, and Norman financial systems while Lyon has been responsible for those comparing Flemish and English financial institutions and the final chapter which attempts to pull together the material and draw some conclusions on the financial institutions of western Europe.

The chronological limitations put upon this study demand explanation. They rest upon good historical reasons. In these four states of western Europe, which were among the first to feel the effects of the eleventh-century economic revival and which first felt the need to develop more efficient systems for the collection and disbursement of revenue, well-organized financial systems arose in the late eleventh and twelfth centuries. By the last quarter of the twelfth century the systems of England, Normandy, and Flanders had achieved a perfection of organization soon to be changed by shift in political power and by new economic demands of the thirteenth century. The Battle of Bouvines had as decisive an effect upon Flemish institutions as did the loss of Normandy upon Norman and English institutions[1]. It is not coincidence that the new forms of taxation in the thirteenth century forced the traditional financial organization of the twelfth century to change. In a period when western Europe rapidly shifted from feudal to non-feudal institutions it was inevitable that financial systems should undergo alteration. Although in the first seventy-five years of the twelfth century the Capetians had no financial machinery to compare with that of their neighbors, it came finally in the last quarter of the century. With the political triumphs of Philip Augustus that so altered Flemish, Norman, and English history came the rise of those French financial institutions which took their definite form in the thirteenth century[2]. While it may never be known, one cannot but wonder how much institutional know-how the Capetian monarchy obtained from its victories in Normandy and Flanders.

[1] *Ibid.*, pp. 60-66, 137-138.

[2] H. Pirenne, *Histoire de Belgique*, I, p. 242: "Du commencement du XIIIe siècle au commencement du XIVe, la France, débarrassée de la rivalité de l'Angleterre et de celle de l'Empire, exerça l'hégémonie en Europe."

Chapter II

FLEMISH FINANCIAL INSTITUTIONS FROM THE ELEVENTH TO THE THIRTEENTH CENTURY

1. *Central Financial Administration*

As a prelude to a comparative study of financial institutions in the twelfth century it is necessary to survey those of Flanders from the eleventh to the thirteenth century. What follows is not a résumé of our present knowledge of the subject but a fresh investigation of the sources conceived on a western European basis from which some new conclusions will emerge[1].

One generally begins the financial history of the county of Flanders with the famous charter granted by Count Robert II on 31 October 1089. By this charter the count appointed as chancellor and "susceptorem et exactorem de omnibus reditibus principatus Flandrie" the provost of the church of St. Donatian located within the confines of the count's castle at Bruges[2]. Although on diplomatic and paleographical grounds the authenticity of this charter has been challenged by some historians[3],

[1] For recent studies on Flemish financial institutions see: R. Monier, *Les institutions financières du comté de Flandre du XIe siècle à 1384* (Paris, 1948); T. Luykx, *De Grafelijke Financiële Bestuursinstellingen en het Grafelijk Patrimonium in Vlaanderen tijdens de Regering van Margareta van Constantinopel (1244-1278)* (Brussels, 1961); Verhulst and Gysseling, *Compte général.* Perroy points out opportunities for comparison of Flemish financial institutions with those of neighboring states in his review of the Verhulst and Gysseling book in *Revue du Nord*, XLIV (1962), 443-446. See also P. Thomas, "La renenghelle de Flandre aux XIIIe et XIVe siècles," *Bull. Comm. Hist. du Nord*, XXXIII (1930), 169; Haskins, *Norman Institutions*, pp. 44-45; B. Lyon, *A Constitutional and Legal History of Medieval England* (New York, 1960), p. 135.

[2] Gysseling and A. C. F. Koch, *Diplomata Belgica ante Annum Millesimum Centesimum Scripta* (Brussels, 1950), Pt. I, no. 170, pp. 295-298.

[3] F. Vercauteren, *Actes des comtes de Flandre 1071-1128* (Brussels, 1938), pp. 24-29; Gysseling and Koch, *Diplomata Belgica*, I, 289-294.

today it is generally considered authentic[1]. Unfortunately most of the research on this charter has ignored its significance for the early financial history of Flanders. While some historians have argued that the appointment of the provost as chancellor of the count had no practical significance for comital finance, others since the time of Henri Pirenne have begun to understand the importance of the provost's being given the function of *susceptor et exactor* as well as chancellor. Pirenne pointed out that as early as 1128 *notarii* appeared as financial technicians of the count and were subordinate to the provost of St. Donatian in his capacity of *susceptor et exactor*[2]. It has subsequently been pointed out that since the middle of the twelfth century a growing number of documents show that the administration of comital finance on both a local and central level was entrusted to *notarii* who acknowledged the provost of St. Donatian as their head and worked under his direction[3]. What is essential is to determine the real significance of the appointment in 1089 of the provost of St. Donatian as *susceptor et exactor*.

In the account of Galbert of Bruges concerning the murder of Count Charles the Good on 2 March 1127 there is an episode that throws light on the treasury of the count[4]. Hiding in the church of St. Donatian where the count lay murdered were a chaplain, three clerics, the *notarius* Fromold Junior, and Arnold the chamberlain, all members of the administration of the count. They are discovered by the murderers who then discuss whether they should kill Fromold Junior, "more intimate with Count Charles than others of the court," or save his life until they

[1] Ganshof, in *Institutions françaises*, I, 381. O. Oppermann has analyzed the content of this charter in an unsuccessful attempt to prove it false (*Untersuchungen zur nordniederländischen Geschichte des 10. bis 13. Jahrhunderts*, Utrecht, 1920, I, 236-245).

[2] H. Pirenne, "La chancellerie et les notaires des comtes de Flandre avant le XIIIᵉ siècle," in *Mélanges Julien Havet* (Paris, 1895), pp. 733-748. See also Vercauteren, *Actes*, pp. lv-lvi; E. Strubbe, in *Revue Belge de Philologie et d'Histoire*, XVIII (1939), 1018; Ganshof, in *Institutions françaises*, I, 381-382.

[3] Ganshof, in *Institutions françaises*, I, 382, 420-421.

[4] Pirenne, *Histoire du meurtre de Charles le Bon comte de Flandre (1127-1128) par Galbert de Bruges* (Paris, 1891), Ch. XVIII, pp. 31-32. See also J. B. Ross, *The Murder of Charles the Good, Count of Flanders, by Galbert of Bruges* (New York, 1960), pp. 127-129.

could extort all the treasure of the count from him and from Arnold the chamberlain[1].

From this passage it is clear that the custody and probably the direction of the comital treasury which, according to Galbert[2], contained enormous amounts of coined and uncoined silver was entrusted in 1127 and probably before to the cleric and *notarius* Fromold Junior and the layman Arnold who was chamberlain. Fromold Junior kept the keys of the treasury; in his capacity as *breviator* he noted receipts and expenditures, probably of the treasury, on an account *(breve);* and he also supplied the count's house at Bruges with grain, wine, and other foodstuffs. Arnold the chamberlain is mentioned as a witness in different charters between 1130 and 1139, and in 1140 there is a reference to his activity in the account of the collector of the *fodermolt* (a rent) at St.-Winoksbergen[3]. On behalf of the chamberlain a messenger came to St.-Winoksbergen to collect the *denarii* of the *fodermolt* which was obviously earmarked for the treasury, administered at that moment by the chamberlain. Because the order to obtain the money came from the cham-

[1] Galbert de Bruges, Ch. XVIII, p. 32 : "Interim consiliabatur Isaac cum Borsiardo, quid melius faceret, utrum ibidem occideret an vitae adhuc reservaret, donec extorquerent ab eo [= Fromoldo] omnem comitis thesaurum simul et ab Arnoldo camerario quem presentem captivaverant." *Ibid.*, Ch. XIX, p. 33: "Verum tamen fuit, quod nullus de curia comiti ita familiaris esset, cum viveret, neque ita carus sicut prefatus Fromoldus." *Ibid.*, Ch. XVIII, p. 31: "Fromoldus junior, notarius et ceteris de curia familiarior comiti Karolo."

[2] *Ibid.*, Ch. XLIX, p. 78: "Nam vere constitit illum Willelmum Iprensem suscepisse de thesauro comitis Karoli Anglicae monetae quingentas libras"; Ch. LXXXV, pp. 129-130: "ut ille captivus insinuaret comiti, qui de canonicis vel laicis obtinuissent a preposito Bertulfo thesaurum . . . Inculpavit ergo decanum Heliam pro trecentis marcis, Litteram canonicum pro ducentis marcis, Robertum custodem ecclesiae pro culcitris et palliis et argento, Radulphum magistrum pro sex scyphis argenteis, Robertum filium Lidgardis pro centum marcis argenti." Pirenne was incorrect to consider Fromold a layman (*Mélanges Julien Havet*, p. 747).

[3] Galbert de Bruges, Ch. XCVII, p. 35: "ex communi consilio prepositi et nepotum ejus et complicum suorum, claves de thesauro comitis a Fromoldo juniore, quem captivum tenebant, requirebant." See also Miraeus-Foppens, *Opera Diplomatica*, II, 679; and the remarks of H. Van Houtte, *Essai sur la civilisation flamande au commencement du XIIe siècle, d'après Galbert de Bruges* (Louvain, 1898), p. 34; E. Strubbe, *Het Fragment van een Grafelijke Rekening van Vlaanderen uit 1140*, in *Mededelingen van de Koninklijke Vlaamse Academie voor Wetenschappen*, Klasse der Letteren, XII (Brussels, 1950), pp. 14-16.

berlain, he may be supposed to rank above the *notarius* who in 1127 shared the administration of the treasury with him. This is a logical conclusion because the chamberlain, as a secular court official, ranked above a *notarius* of the count. Apart from Fromold's intimacy with Count Charles the Good, which was based on strictly personal grounds, a notary was simply an official placed at the disposal of the chamberlain because of his ability to read, write, and calculate, an ability that the chamberlain as a layman probably did not possess. Such evidence proves that at least until 1140 the *camera* had an essential if not a central role in the financial administration of the count of Flanders.

In addition to the chamberlain Arnold, Galbert of Bruges mentions two other chamberlains, Gervase of Praet and Isaac, who probably were court officials of the same rank as Arnold[1]. This reference plus others from charters of the count indicates the existence of several chamberlains[2]. It is clear, however, that these two chamberlains had no connection with the administration of the treasury but worked only for the *camera*. One may conclude, therefore, that within the *camera* some specialization had been achieved by 1127. That a notary was put at the disposal of the chamberlain Arnold may also be considered as a step in the development of a specialized accounting office within the *camera*.

The existence of a treasury as part of the *camera* raises the problem of the authority of the provost-chancellor who since 1089 had been *susceptor et exactor* of the incomes of Flanders. The central financial administration of the count thus seems to have been composed of two parts, a fact hitherto unnoticed by historians. This division is shown in a charter granted by Count Robert II in 1101 to the chapter of St. Donatian. Referring to the charter of 1089, the count declared that he desired to endow the church of St. Donatian, "inter cetera dispensationis mee officia," with certain privileges[3]. This clearly means that in addition to the church of St. Donatian other branches of the

---

[1] Galbert de Bruges, Chs. XVI, XXVI, XXVIII.
[2] Vercauteren, *Actes*, pp. lxxx-lxxxiii.
[3] *Ibid.*, no. 26, pp. 77-82.

comital government, such as the *camera* or at least its financial department, were charged with the administration of the finances.

The exact competence of the provost-chancellor in financial matters can be determined in part with the help of Galbert of Bruges. We learn from him that the provost of St. Donatian, although having no control over the treasury of the count, was entrusted with the custody of the "brevia et notationes de redditibus comitis." That this function was of capital importance is proved by the fact that the provost, during the troubles which followed the murder of Count Charles the Good, took particular care of these documents with the intent of putting them at the disposal of William of Ypres whom he favored for the countship[1]. Obviously knowledge of the annual revenues due him was essential for a new count if he was to collect and control them.

We learn more about the authority of the provost from another passage of Galbert. When on Ascension Day 1128 the *berquarii* and *custodes curtium* came to see the new count, William Clito, staying with his troops at Oudenburg, to render their periodical payments, the count had to send a messenger to Bruges to find and bring to Oudenburg a *notarius* called Basilius without whose help the count was not able to calculate the payments of these officials[2]. Undoubtedly Basilius was a notary in the service of the provost. The account of the *fodermolt* of St.-Winoksbergen buttresses this argument because it clearly shows the chamberlain receiving the money and the provost as responsible for the account[3].

The provost-chancellor was entrusted, therefore, with the keeping of the accounts of the fixed revenues of the count and with control over current expenditures of local rent-collecting centers. The chamberlain, on the other hand, was entrusted with the treasury; he received the money and made payments for

[1] Galbert de Bruges, Ch. XXXV, p. 57.
[2] *Ibid.*, Ch. CXII, p. 159: "Pridie kalendas junii, in die Ascensionis Domini, ex Oldenburg misit quendam monachum nomine Basilium comes Willelmus, precipiens notario suo Basilio, ut ad se festinaret, eo quod in presentiam suam berquarii et custodes curtium et reddituum suorum rationem debitorum suorum reddituri venissent."
[3] Strubbe, *Fragment*, p. 19.

the count. To put it simply, the chamberlain was a cashier; the provost-chancellor, an accountant.

Did, however, the control of the provost-chancellor extend over all the revenues of the count? In the documents of the twelfth and thirteenth centuries the provost is never said to be receiving money apart from certain revenues due him as an allowance for his office. In the general accounts *(Grote Brieven)* controlled by the provost the sums due from the local collectors are always said to have been paid to the count except where the entries pertain to the allowance of the provost for his office[1]. The preservation of the collector's account of the *fodermolt* received from St.-Winoksbergen in 1140 among the archives of the provost proves that the provost controlled payments made by this collector to the chamberlain[2]. One may suppose that the chamberlain delivered to the local collector at St.-Winoksbergen a receipt, as for example a tally, which at the end of the year was presented to the provost. Indeed the examination of tallies is mentioned in the thirteenth century as a privilege of the provost[3]. Had the provost, moreover, received cash revenues, he would not have tried so obstinately in 1127 to get hold of the count's treasure. It would seem, therefore, that the title of *susceptor et exactor* bestowed on the provost in 1089 must be understood in a restrictive sense, that is, that the provost was simply an officer responsible for the collection and supervision of all the accounts of the local collectors, for which purpose he possessed some coercive jurisdiction. It was the chamberlain, however, who received the money. For the present it can only be said that the authority of the provost extended only over those revenues of which he kept the *brevia et annotationes*, that is, the fixed and regular revenues of the count.

From the *Grote Brief* of 1187 we first learn definitely how the count's revenues were collected[4]. There were offices in the

---

[1] Ghent, Rijksarchief, Fonds Gaillard, no. 72*bis*: *Ius Notarii Flandrie*.

[2] Strubbe, *Fragment*, pp. 15-16.

[3] From charter of Countess Jeanne in 1233 printed in L. A. Warnkoenig, *Flandrische Staats- und Rechtsgeschichte* (Tübingen, 1839), III, 2, no. CX, p. 185: "Similiter pro vadiis [prepositus] habebit, quod rationabiliter expenderit in fractione dicarum, quae theutonice kerlistoch dicuntur."

[4] Verhulst and Gysseling, *Compte général*, pp. 77-101, 122-128.

most important administrative centers of the county *(châtelle-nies)* and in smaller exploitation-centers encompassing a group of the count's manors where the count's revenues from these regions were centralized by a receiver. If several of these offices were established in one locality or within one circumscription, there was some specialization in the revenues collected as, for example, corn, animal produce, dairy produce, and money, so that the offices were distinguished by the names *spicaria, lardaria, vaccaria,* and *brevia.* In Bruges, where the central organs of the financial administration were located, there were other specialized offices known as the *magna brevia* and *brevia camere.* Though most of the revenues of the local offices came from the count's domain, some came from tolls, mints, jurisdictional rights, and special taxes levied by the count as ruler of the county; these latter revenues were rare, however, in the general account of 1187. During the twelfth century these revenues were collected by special receivers, whose accounts were not incorporated in the *Grote Brief,* as was the case for some tolls collected by *telonearii,* for some incomes from mints collected by *monetarii,* for profits of justice collected towards the end of the twelfth century by the bailiffs, and for revenues from the sale of the comital waste lands. These revenues only became important in the twelfth century with the economic revival and the centralization of comital government[1].

During the second half of the twelfth century the more lucrative revenues were no longer collected by the *spicaria, lardaria,* and *brevia* but by particular receivers. Although all revenues except for certain tolls and taxes had to be collected locally before being turned in to a central treasury, the general evolution of the later twelfth century was toward financial

[1] The receipts from the toll at Bruges are not entered in the *Grote Brief.* This is also the case for the toll of Bapaume upon which the count of Flanders assigned 500 *l.* to the count of Hainault (L. Vanderkindere, *La chronique de Gislebert de Mons,* Brussels, 1904, p. 99 and no. 4). On these other incomes see R. Richebé, *Essai sur le régime financier de la Flandre avant l'institution de la chambre des comptes de Lille* (Paris, 1889), p. 89; Ganshof, in *Institutions françaises,* I, 423; H. Nowé, *Les baillis comtaux de Flandre* (Brussels, 1929), pp. 174-177; Strubbe, *Egidius van Breedene. Grafelijk Ambtenaar en Stichter van de Abdij Spermalie* (Bruges, 1942), p. 42; Luykx, *Grafelijke Financiële Bestuursinstellingen,* pp. 48-52.

centralization. It is therefore probable that from the early twelfth century there were two distinct types of comital revenue, that collected by territorial receivers of the *spicaria* and *brevia* and that which went directly to the treasury. In general the former comprised the fixed and regular revenues of the count; the latter, the casual revenues. By the thirteenth century with the manorial economy yielding to the money economy the fixed revenues accounted for yearly in the *Grote Brief* became less important than the casual.

That the authority of the provost-chancellor extended only to the yearly audit of the receipts and expenditures for which the collectors of the *spicaria* and *brevia* were responsible and which were recorded in the *Grote Brief* accounts for the eclipse of this officer in the late twelfth and thirteenth centuries. Meanwhile one can assume that the chamberlain who received all the old comital incomes as well as the new made possible by the reviving money economy increased his authority. We do know that in the first half of the thirteenth century a cleric acted as receiver of the count and was considered the head of a new accounting office[1]. It seems certain that this cleric was first in the service of the chamberlain and superseded him when the financial administration apparently had to be reorganized to handle the new incomes. About the middle of the twelfth century the functions of all the old court officials, including the chamberlain, became purely honorary and hereditary[2]. The cleric-notary thus became the head of a treasury independent from the *camera*[3]. This new treasurer developed an administration that replaced the old accounting-office of the provost, a development which led to the treasurer's becoming the principal financial officer in the second half of the thirteenth century[4].

[1] Luykx, *Grafelijke Financiële Bestuursinstellingen*, pp. 52-62.

[2] Ganshof, in *Institutions françaises*, I, 379-380.

[3] The financial competence of the *camera* was henceforth limited to receipts and expenditures of the *brevia camere*, an office at that time probably organized as a part of the *redeninge*.

[4] We disagree with Luykx that these changes were made without protest from the provost-chancellor. The document in question was not an official record of the provost-chancellor's privileges but a defense against the loss of his authority (Luykx, *Grafelijke Financiële Bestuursinstellingen*, p. 64).

2. *Territorial Administration of Comital Finance*

Having traced the development of the central financial administration down to the thirteenth century let us now turn to the relation between the provost-chancellor and the system of *spicaria* and *brevia*. The oldest centers for the collection of revenue were established at *castra*, generally erected between the beginning of the tenth and the middle of the eleventh centuries[1]. It may be assumed that the oldest *spicaria* (Bruges, Ghent, Douai, Veurne, St.-Winoksbergen, St.-Omer) were organized along with these *castra*. In regions where the landed possessions of the counts were scattered or where they were not organized in manorial units, *castra* were like the centers of large Carolingian *villae*, serving as autonomous rent-collecting centers within the *spicaria* system or even within the circumscription of a *spicarium* itself (i.e., Roeselare, Harelbeke, Maldegem, Coudescure, Hazebrouck, Watou)[2].

During the countships of Baldwin IV and Baldwin V *castra* became the centers of new administrative circumscriptions, the *châtellenies*, controlled by *châtelains*. At this time the counts apparently restricted the financial authority of the *châtelains* by removing the *spicaria* from their control[3]. This can be seen in the administrative reforms which the count instituted in the *châtellenie* of Ypres between 1126 and 1132[4]. During the eleventh century Ypres had been the center of a large comital manor where there was a *castrum* and a *spicarium*. Originally a part of the *châtellenie* of St.-Omer, this manor was organized as a

[1] Verhulst and Gysseling, *Compte général*, pp. 90-101.

[2] L. Voet, "De Graven van Vlaanderen en hun Domein," *Wetenschappelijke Tijdingen*, VII (1942), Col. 25-32; A. C. F. Koch, *De Rechterl'jke Organisatie van het Graafschap Vlaanderen tot in de 13ᵉ Eeuw* (Antwerp, 1950), pp. 10 ff.

[3] The *castrum* was not part of the fief of the *châtelain* (Ganshof, in *Institutions françaises*, p. 401). *Châtelains* did, however, administer and hold in fief important comital revenues (W. Blommaert, *Les châtelains de Flandre*, Ghent, 1915, pp. 190-191, 195, 221). The *châtelains* of St.-Omer controlled the *foragium*, but at Douai and Lille the profits from this right were collected by the receivers of the *spicarium* (Verhulst and Gysseling, *Compte général*, pp. 157-168). Some *châtelains* controlled the incomes from markets and tolls.

[4] Koch, *Rechterlijke Organisatie*, pp. 95-104.

separate *châtellenie* in the second half of the eleventh century. The office of *châtelain*, however, was entrusted to the domanial reeve *(laicus prepositus)* who thus held both offices. Because the *châtelain* of Ypres was involved in the murder of Count Charles the Good (1127), he was removed and his two functions were divided. Henceforth the keeper of the *spicarium* was distinct from the *châtelain*.

What kind of officer, then, was entrusted with the collection of the revenues of the *spicarium?* For a long time historians have adhered to the opinion of Pirenne that the *notarii* were appointed receivers of all local rent-collecting centers[1]. This opinion, however, is not substantiated by the evidence. First it must be noted that about 1177-1187 only some local rent-collecting centers were headed by *notarii;* most were administered by laymen, including members of the nobility such as the widow of the *châtelain* of Douai, who was receiver of the *spicarium* at Douai, and her son Peter, who was receiver of the *brevia* of Lécluse. Other laymen collecting revenues were the *venatores* who administered the *brevia* of Aalter and the *lardarium* of Bruges; such *servientes* of the count as the receiver of the *spicarium* at Ypres and the receiver of the *spicarium* at Hazebrouck; a certain cleric Peter who was bailiff and comital receiver at Hesdin; *prepositi* at Bapaume, Halluin, and perhaps Lille; a *dispensator* who was receiver of the *spicarium* at Courtrai; and a *preco* who was receiver at Deinze. Though one might suppose that these laymen had recently superseded the *notarii* as receivers, this does not seem to be true. This change really took place at the end of the twelfth century and the beginning of the thirteenth[2].

There is however evidence showing that since the end of the eleventh century *notarii* had not administered all the local rent-collecting centers. The *spicarium* of Ypres, for example, was administered by a *prepositus* up to 1127. We do not know what official replaced him, but it may have been the son of the former *prepositus* who, like his father, continued to bear the title of

---

[1] Pirenne, in *Mélanges Julien Havet*, p. 744.

[2] Verhulst and Gysseling, *Compte général*, pp. 105-119; Koch, *Rechterlijke Organisatie*, pp. 85, 144; Luykx, *Grafelijke Financiële Bestuursinstellingen*, pp. 36-38.

châtelain or *vicecomes* though he may in fact have been a notary[1]. If he was indeed a notary, it was by accident, because he was appointed receiver for merely personal reasons. This means that the office of receiver of the *spicarium* of Ypres was not deliberately entrusted to a *notarius*, a conclusion supported by the vagueness of the title borne by the receiver of this *spicarium* in 1161. At this time he is not called *notarius* but "[ille] qui Ypris ministerium victualium nostrorum tenuerit"[2]. This conclusion is corroborated by the fact that in 1187 the receiver of the Ypres *spicarium*, Henricus de Paskendale, was no notary, but bore the title of *serviens comitis* and *justiciarius Yprensis*. He was indeed the precursor of the bailiff, and perhaps the first bailiff of Ypres[3].

The case of Ypres does not stand alone. Simon, *dispensator* at St.-Omer in 1092, 1093, and 1128[4], and charged with the payment to the abbey of Ham of an annual rent of 100 *s*., has been hitherto considered a *notarius*[5]. What is striking, however, is that his successor Robert is mentioned in 1138 as *dispensator*[6]. And yet none of the twelfth-century *dispensatores* have been proved to be notaries[7]. The *dispensator* of St.-Omer, who administered the *officium* at St.-Omer from 1092 to 1138 must therefore have been an official of another type; he was in fact a local seneschal. Not only is *dispensator* synonymous with seneschal and their functions identical, but there is a further

---

[1] Koch, *Rechterlijke Organisatie*, pp. 101, 104.

[2] L. Gilliodts-Van Severen, *Coutume de la ville et châtellenie de Furnes* (Brussels, 1897), no. III, pp. 20-22; P. Thomas, *Textes historiques sur Lille et le Nord de la France avant 1789* (Lille, 1936), II, no. 83, pp. 259-262. At this time the receiver of Ypres did not have to be a *notarius* and he certainly was not a local seneschal.

[3] Verhulst and Gysseling, *Compte général*, p. 114; Nowé, *Baillis comtaux*, p. 44; Koch, *Rechterlijke Organisatie*, p. 202.

[4] Vercauteren, *Actes*, pp. lii, 37.

[5] *Ibid.*, pp. l, 37.

[6] Unpublished charter of Count Thierry of about 1138 to abbey of Ham in the archives of the Marquis de Beauffort at Brussels: MS. Hannedouche, II, p. 70. Noted by A. Du Chesne, in *Histoire généalogique des maisons de Guines, d'Ardres, de Gand et de Coucy* (Paris, 1631), Preuves, p. 212.

[7] E. Warlop, "De *dispensator* van de Graaf van Vlaanderen (1093-einde 13ᵉ Eeuw)," *Verslagen en Mededelingen van De Leiegouw*, V (1963), pp. 31-43.

argument in favor of this view[1]. Count Thierry of Flanders, granting privileges in 1160 to the inhabitants of the *villes neuves* of Berquin and Steenwerck, ordained that their offences should be judged by the *dapifer* on the *placitum generale*[2]. The count evidently did not mean the *dapifer Flandrie*, but the local *dapifer*[3] who could be none other than the receiver of the *spicarium* of St.-Omer because Berquin and Steenwerck were at that time part of this circumscription[4]. Finally, it should be noted that Reinoud of Aire, *dispensator* in 1163, became bailiff of St.-Omer in 1191[5]. As at Ypres, therefore, the receiver of the *spicarium* at St.-Omer was originally a local seneschal *(dispensator-dapifer)* who eventually became the bailiff[6]. At Courtrai also, the *spicarium* may have been administered by a *dispensator* as early as the middle of the twelfth century. Between 1151 and 1164 a certain Rogerus *dispensator* is mentioned in several charters. We can identify him with Rogerus, receiver of the *spicarium* at Courtrai in 1187, or with his son, because during the first half of the thirteenth century a Roger [of Bellegem] is not only receiver of the *spicarium* at Courtrai but also holds the hereditary title of *dispensator*[7]. From the five *dispensatores* of the twelfth century noted above, three can be identified as receivers of *spicaria*, and it is not impossible that the other two were also[8].

[1] Ganshof, in *Institutions françaises*, I, 379, notes that *senescalus, dapifer,* and *dispensator* were synonymous before the thirteenth century.

[2] D. Van Derveeghde, "Note sur une charte originale octroyée par le comte de Flandre à ses tenanciers de Berquin et de Steenwerck (1160)," *Bulletin de la Commission Royale d'Histoire*, CXVIII (1953), 330-331.

[3] Koch, *Rechterlijke Organisatie*, p. 200; Ganshof, in *Institutions françaises*, I, 380.

[4] In 1187 Berquin and Steenwerck were under the *spicarium* of Bailleul. In 1160 Bailleul had been split off from the *spicarium* of St.-Omer (Verhulst and Gysseling, *Compte général*, pp. 178-179, 96).

[5] A. Van Lokeren, *Chartes et documents de l'abbaye de Saint-Pierre au Mont-Blandin à Gand* (Ghent, 1868), I, no. 283, p. 162; Nowé, *Baillis comtaux*, p. 56.

[6] Koch, *Rechterlijke Organisatie*, pp. 199-200.

[7] Warlop, in *Verslagen van De Leiegouw*, V, 33-35; Verhulst and Gysseling, *Compte général*, p. 116; Luykx, *Grafelijke Financiële Bestuursinstellingen*, p. 38.

[8] A certain Richard noted as *dispensator* or *dapifer* may perhaps be identified as the receiver of the *spicarium* at St.-Winoksbergen in 1187. See the references in H. Coppieters Stochove, *Régestes de Thierri d'Alsace* (Ghent, 1902), and *Régestes de Philippe d'Alsace* (Ghent, 1906); Verhulst and Gysseling, *Compte général*, p. 115.

It has been concluded that as early as the first half of the twelfth century and perhaps even at the end of the eleventh *prepositi*, *dapiferi*, or *dispensatores* may have been receivers of local rent-collecting centers[1]. We believe also that they formed the majority of the local receivers and that they were only gradually replaced in most places by *notarii*.

In the first place *notarii* only appear frequently in the records towards the end of the eleventh century, and not until the reign of Count Thierry (1128-1168) are they mentioned explicitly as the count's local receivers[2]. Secondly, it should be pointed out that the fiscal circumscriptions of Harelbeke and Cassel were called *prefectura* and *castellatura* already in 1075 and 1085[3]. This presumes that the heads of these fiscal circumscriptions were originally *prepositi* or *castellani*[4]. A. Koch has drawn the parallel between Ypres and Harelbeke. At the end of the eleventh century Harelbeke was an important domanial unit, headed by a *prepositus (laicus)* who at the same time probably acted as receiver of this fiscal unit. Later in the twelfth century his fiscal duties were given to a *notarius*[5]. In the third place it is striking that during the twelfth century *notarii* are found as receivers in the three main *châtellenies* of Bruges, Veurne, and Ghent; in rent-collecting centers of recent creation such as the *census* of Diksmuide and Courtrai; in the centers of *châtellenies* of recent creation such as Aire and Cassel; and in former domanial units such as Harelbeke and Roeselare where the counts as private landowners could more easily carry through reforms. Lastly, the

[1] See above, pp. 21-23. This was probably true for the *prepositi* serving in 1187 as receivers at Bapaume, Lille, Halluin, and Hesdin; for the *preco* acting as receiver at Deinze; and for the *venatores* serving in 1187 as receivers of the *brevia* and *lardarium* at Aalter and Bruges.

[2] Vercauteren, *Actes*, pp. l-lii; Nowé, *Baillis comtaux*, p. 31. The following quotation comes from an unpublished charter of Count Thierry in 1157: "preposito Brugensi et notariis meis qui Furnis redditus meos colligunt predictam pecuniam nuntio sacrarum monialium sine dilatione solvere firmiter iniungo" (Archives Départementales of Maine-et-Loire, no. 237 H 1). It was only after Philip was associated with his father in the government of Flanders in 1157 that *notarii* are cited frequently in the charters.

[3] Vercauteren, *Actes*, no. 3, p. 6; no. 6, p. 18.

[4] This was the case at Harelbeke where, as at Ypres, he was called *laicus prepositus* (Koch, *Rechterlijke Organisatie*, pp. 142-143).

[5] See preceding note and Verhulst and Gysseling, *Compte général*, p. 110.

collecting of the comital revenues within fiscal circumscriptions was entrusted to *precones, prepositi,* or *villici,* all officers who had mainly judicial functions[1]. Obviously the head of these officials within a given circumscription was originally a judicial officer with authority over finance. In large circumscriptions like the *châtellenie* of Ypres this officer was the *châtelain;* in smaller circumscriptions like Harelbeke, Lille, and Bapaume this officer was the *prepositus.* Even *notarii* continued to be entrusted with judicial functions[2].

Besides these fiscal circumscriptions, other rent-collecting centers were administered by local officials called *dispensatores, dapiferi,* and *venatores* whom the counts began gradually to replace at the end of the eleventh century with *notarii.* The objective of the counts was to keep these local collectors from becoming too powerful and from making their offices heritable and feudal. Except on the strictly local level where *precones, prepositi,* and *villici* continued to collect the comital revenues, the mandate of these officials was therefore limited to merely judicial matters with the *notarii,* who were clerics and non-vassals, becoming the principal financial officers[3]. Though at first this reform only succeeded in the domains that were large and where the counts could interfere with the appointment of officials, by the middle of the twelfth century *notarii* were the principal receivers of the comital income.

In the second half of the twelfth century the *notarii* in turn yielded to another type of financial officer—noble laymen who held their offices in fief[4]. This feudalization of the *spicaria* and *brevia* was complete except for some rent-collecting centers administered by *clerici* which the counts retained under their direct authority. *Notarii* were also replaced in the central administration, this time by *clerici.* Often it meant only a change in title because some *notarii* are known to have become *clerici*[5].

This change in local financial administration is explicable by

---

[1] *Ibid.,* pp. 103-112; Ganshof, in *Institutions françaises,* I, 402.
[2] Nowé, *Baillis comtaux,* pp. 31, 36.
[3] *Ibid.,* p. 36.
[4] Luykx, *Grafelijke Financiële Bestuursinstellingen,* pp. 36-38.
[5] Strubbe, *Egidius van Breedene,* pp. 37-46.

the decrease of the old revenues of the *spicaria* and *brevia* and by the development of a new administration under the chamberlain headed by *clerici* responsible for new revenues collected outside the *spicaria-brevia* system, as well as by the development during the last quarter of the twelfth century of a new financial and judicial officer—the bailiff[1].

Although H. Nowé has proved that in some cases *notarii* became bailiffs and that the judicial tasks of the *notarii* fell to the bailiffs, we can extend his thesis to some receivers who were not *notarii*[2]. As we have seen, the receiver of the *spicarium* at Ypres in 1187 *(justiciarius Yprensis)*, though not a *notarius*, was the first bailiff of Ypres. We have also seen that the *dispensator* of the *spicarium* at St.-Omer became a bailiff about the year 1191 and that the receiver of the *brevia* of Hesdin in 1187 was also a bailiff. The Nowé thesis may therefore be expanded to say that the first bailiffs of the counts were generally chosen from the receivers of *spicaria* and *brevia*, whether they be *notarius*, *dispensator*, *clericus*, or *serviens comitis*, that while still serving as receivers they began to perform the duties of a pre-bailiff, and that soon they lost most of their financial duties and became simply a bailiff[3]. They retained, however, several duties performed formerly as receivers, such as the payment of current casual expenses. Naturally, therefore, these expenses, which appeared in the *Grote Brief* of 1187, do not appear in the next extant *Grote Brief* of 1255[4].

As with the *notarii* one hundred years before, the bailiffs evolved in response to the comital desire for better control over local administration. The counts wanted officials whose offices were non-heritable and non-feudal and whom they could replace at will. Feudal custom and heritability were so strong that some *notarii* had succeeded in making their offices feudal[5]. The non-

---

[1] *Ibid.*, pp. 41-42.

[2] Nowé, *Baillis comtaux*, pp. 38-43.

[3] *Ibid.*, pp. 174-181.

[4] It is possible that among the receipts of the bailiffs which were both judicial and manorial some had been collected by receivers of the *spicaria* and *brevia* and had not been entered with the ordinary revenues in the *Grote Brief* (Verhulst and Gysseling, *Compte général*, p. 49).

[5] Verhulst, "Twee Oorkonden van Filips van de Elzas voor het Leprozenhuis,

feudal bailiffs replaced the *notarii* and, though their functions were primarily judicial, they retained some financial competence and were considered in the same category as the other receivers of the count who stood outside the *spicaria-brevia* system such as the *telonearii* and *monetarii*. If the counts permitted local receivers of the old comital income to hold their offices in fief, it was because this income constantly declined in value.

When the provost of St. Donatian was appointed in 1089 *susceptor et exactor* of the income from the comital domain, he was also given a *magisterium* over the various officials connected with finance on a central and local level[1]. But it was not his authority as *magisterium* which gave the provost-chancellor supervision over the accounts of the *notarii* and other income-collecting officers of the count in the annual audit sessions known as the *redeninge* (French, *renenghe*).

By the thirteenth century when we begin to know something about the *redeninge* it was a meeting held once a year around 24 June[2] with the purpose of auditing the accounts of the receivers of the *spicaria* and *brevia* and of adjudicating disputes connected with the comital revenue not able to be settled on a local level[3]. This assembly was composed of all the receivers who administered *spicaria* or *brevia* summoned by written order of the provost who presided over the audit[4]. When the *redeninge* acted as a court the provost presided only in the absence of the

bevattende nieuwe Gegevens betreffende de Geschiedenis van Gent in de 12ᵉ Eeuw," *Handelingen van de Maatschappij voor Geschiedenis en Oudheidkunde te Gent*, new ser., XIII (1959), 23.

[1] Ganshof, in *Institutions françaises*, I, 381; Strubbe, *Egidius van Breedene*, pp. 32-37.

[2] C. P. Serrure, *Cartulaire de Saint-Bavon* (Ghent, 1836-1840), no. 231: "in ratiocinio beati Johannis Baptiste" (1241); Luykx, *Grafelijke Financiële Bestuursinstellingen*, no. 100, p. 419: "in ratiociniis Insulensibus anno Domini 1273 circa Nativitatem beati Johannis Baptiste observandis." It is not certain that this was a fixed date at the end of the twelfth century. In 1187 the *redeninge* was held 1 to 9 June. In any event the *redeninge* was always held after Ascension Day.

[3] In 1187 the *redeninge* was at Ypres but in the thirteenth century was held more often at Lille.

[4] This was the case in the thirteenth century although it is possible that in the twelfth century the composition of this court was broader (Ganshof, in *Institutions françaises*, I, 393).

count[1]. The count was in fact the presiding officer of the *redeninge*, although in practice he left this task to the provost. This and the fact that the *notarii* in the twelfth century and the *feodales homines ratiocinatores* in the thirteenth were members of both the *redeninge* and the count's *curia* shows that the *redeninge* was but a specialized financial session of the *curia*[2].

Until 1157 financial matters were treated in general sessions of the *curia*[3]. Specialization came gradually with the need to audit the accounts of the *notarii* and with the old court officials' becoming honorific. Sometime before 1190, and definitely by 1187, the *redeninge* functioned as a specialized session of the *curia*[4]. Perhaps antecedents of the *redeninge* may be seen in the local audit-sessions, also called *redeninge*, held during the third quarter of the twelfth century. In 1167, 1170, and 1178 meetings of the local *redeninge* were held at Veurne. Summoned by the provost and presided over by him, the local receivers of Veurne and its neighborhood met to settle disputes over the count's domain and to conduct transactions related to the comital landed possessions[5]. Though mention of such sessions is limited to Veurne, it is possible that such local sessions were held in other places[6]. Can one not suppose that about the same time the central *redeninge* modeled on these local *redeninge* and composed of

[1] Gilliodts-Van Severen, *Coutume de la prévôté de Bruges* (Brussels, 1887), II, no. XXV, pp. 49-50: "Item omnes receptores Flandrie debent esse homines sui [sc. prepositi]; nec debent convocari, nec venire debent ad ratiocinia nisi vocati per litteras ipsius prepositi; nec debent computare nisi coram ipso, et debet presidere in judicio ratiocinii et submonere judicantes in absentia comitis; in presentia autem comitis debet cum aliis judicare; pertinet etiam ad prepositum taxare bladum et avenam et cetera que recipere debent receptores. . ."

[2] This conclusion is supported by Ganshof, in *Institutions françaises*, I, 393.

[3] A charter of Count Thierry making a grant of a rent on the comital domain to the abbey of Fontevrault in 1157 and containing instructions to the provost and the *notarii* as to the payment of this rent is said to have been issued "coram multis baronibus comitis," among whom figure the provost, the chamberlain, and several *notarii* (Archives Départementales of Maine-et-Loire, no. 237 H. 1).

[4] Ganshof, in *Institutions françaises*, I, 393; Verhulst and Gysseling, *Compte général*, pp. 119-121, 41-47.

[5] Verhulst and Gysseling, *Compte général*, p. 120. In a charter of Robert, provost of St. Donatian, to the abbey of St. Bertin in 1170 appears the phrase "sicut . . . in mea ac ratiocinatorum Furnensium audientia recognoverint" (Warnkoenig, *Flandrische Staats- und Rechtsgeschichte*, III, 2, no. LXVII).

[6] It is also significant that a *scaccarium* was located here.

28

ratiocinatores supremi came into existence? How the accounts were audited before the existence of the *redeninge* is a matter of speculation. We can only suggest that judicial questions were settled by the count's *curia*.

3. Exploitation of the Comital Domain

With the *Grote Brief* of 1187 now in our possession it is possible to understand the exploitation of the comital domain. Comparing the *Grote Brief* of 1187 with that of 1255, one sees a striking fact: the majority of receipts and expenditures remain unchanged, a situation which cannot be explained by the fact that by 1255 most offices of receiver had been feudalized. Most expenditures which remained unchanged represented fixed rents granted by the counts on certain revenues in the form of tithes *(redecimae)*, money fiefs *(feoda)*, or alms *(elemosinae)*[1].

We have little evidence relating to comital receipts. That most expenditures in the *Grote Brieven* of 1187 and 1255 remained fixed suggests that the receipts must also have been invariable. But how does one explain this uniformity of receipts? In the account of 1187 certain sums are accompanied by the notation *hoc anno*[2]. This would suggest that the sums so marked could change from year to year. This does not mean, however, that they necessarily did, or that other sums not so marked were necessarily fixed and invariable. While this evidence is of no help, it is significant that in the *Grote Brief* a large number of receipts in money and in kind are in round figures. The following examples of receipts in kind are typical:

Coudescura: ([3])	caput eius tritici	50 h.
	caput avene	450 h.
	galline	25
	ova	250
Hasabroc: ([4])	caput eius tritici	12 1/2 m⁰ (= 100 h.)
	caput avene	700 h.
	galline	40
	ova	400

[1] Verhulst and Gysseling, *Compte général*, pp. 128-137.
[2] *Ibid.*, pp. 43, 46.
[3] *Ibid.*, p. 160.
[4] *Ibid.*

Ypris: [1]	caput eius tritici ex Duvenhof	12 1/2 m⁰ ($=$ 100 h.)
	ex Hersela	10 h.
	caput avene... ex Duvenhof	700 h.
	ex Hersela	40 h.
	galline ex Ypra et Diccabusc	40
	ex Duvenhof	40
	ova ex Ypra et Diccabusc	400
	ex Duvenhof	400
Gandavum: [2]	caput avene ex Haltra	400 h.
	ex Roingem	400 h. (hoc anno)
	ex Somergem	200 h. paratum
		200 h. imparatum

Similar cases can be found in the accounts of Lille and Hesdin, of the *spicarium* and the *lardarium* at St.-Winoksbergen, of the *spicarium* at Diksmuide, and of the *lardarium* at Veurne. It is striking that the figures quoted above are either invariable from one place to another or that there exist arithmetical proportions. We see these proportions between *galline* and *ova* (*ova* = *galline* $\times$ 100) and between the figures for *triticum* and *avena* (for example at Hazebrouck and Ypres: *triticum: avena* = 1/7)[3]. Apart from the suggestion that these arithmetical proportions facilitated the collection of certain revenues, it is obvious that the round figures did not represent the sum of renders in kind due from comital tenants[4]. It must be concluded that these round figures represented fixed payments which had to be rendered annually by local collectors to the regional receivers. Many receipts in money were also expressed in round figures. This was usually the case for receipts of the count from tolls, mints, judicial profits, and sometimes from offices *(ex praepositura, ex preposito)*[5].

That these incomes were expressed in round figures shows that they were not received directly from tenants but were lumped together by local receivers prior to receipt at regional centers. While this means that some large manors *(curtes)* were no longer managed directly, direct exploitation still existed on

[1] *Ibid.*, p. 185.

[2] *Ibid.*, p. 143.

[3] *Ibid.*, p. 188: St.-Winoksbergen *(lardarium)*.

[4] Apropos of this conclusion see the remark of F. W. Maitland, *Domesday Book and Beyond* (Fontana Library, London, 1960), p. 184.

[5] For examples see Verhulst and Gysseling, *Compte général*, pp. 142, 146, 156-158, 163, 167, 173, 178, 181.

the comital domain in 1187, on, for example, certain *curtes* within the circumscriptions of Lillers, Lens, Hesdin, and Aalst, and perhaps on the *grangiae* at Lécluse, Bapaume, and Geraardsbergen[1]. No evidence, however, shows the legal arrangements for farming out the comital revenue to receivers. There are three possibilities: revenues were farmed out either for life or a fixed term, they were let out at a quit-rent *(cens)*, or they were granted in fief. Whatever the method used made little difference; this probably explains why there is no mention of the system used even when comital finance underwent radical change at the end of the twelfth and the early thirteenth centuries[2].

Despite the silence of the records there is some argument for the farming of the revenues. The toll of St.-Omer, which in 1187 no longer was audited at the *redeninge*, had been farmed in 1128 by William Clito to the inhabitants of St.-Omer *in perpetuo censu* in return for a yearly sum of 100 *s*[3]. Though a quit-rent was perpetual the word *perpetuus* was nevertheless placed in the charter. Like J. F. Niermeyer we consider this transaction as creating a fee-farm, a conclusion supported by several thirteenth-century texts[4]. In a document of 1233 concerning the rights of the provost-chancellor a distinction is made between the count's revenues which "temporaliter ad censum concedentur" and other revenues[5]. Here *census* clearly has the meaning not of quit-rent but of a fixed-term lease. We can infer that this type of farm was of recent origin. In the *renenghelle* account of 1296 the *censes* entered separately next to the revenues from *spicaria* and *brevia* and next to the *rentes hors renenghe* were likewise short-term leases of various revenues[6]. This type of farm was used especially with tolls during the thirteenth century, and in the twelfth century was even used for revenues

---

[1] *Ibid.*, pp. 161-165, 193, 158-159, 192.

[2] Though numerous changes occurred in the late twelfth and early thirteenth centuries they are not reflected in the *Grote Brief* of 1255 which differs little from that of 1187.

[3] A. Giry, *Histoire de la ville de Saint-Omer* (Paris, 1877), p. 377, no. 4.

[4] J. F. Niermeyer, *Mediae Latinitatis Lexicon Minus* (Leiden, 1955), II, 168, v. *census*, 5, e.

[5] Warnkoenig, *Flandrische Staats- und Rechtsgeschichte*, III, 2, no. CX.

[6] Luykx, *Grafelijke Financiële Bestuursinstellingen*, pp. 51-52.

31

audited at the *redeninge*. In the *censes* of the *renenghelle* of 1296 there is, for example, an entry traceable to the *Grote Brief* of 1187: "de le cense de Vrasene en Waize fait par Baudouin le Ghent et fina li cense a le Nativite S. Jehan Baptiste en lan LXXXXVI dont li somme est par an 12 *s.*"[1] This entry undoubtedly refers to the receipt *ex censu Frasena 6 s. Andwerpenses* in the *Grote Brief* of 1187, which is identical because *1 d. Andwerpensis = 2 d. Flandrenses*[2]. The revenues from the Waas circumscription, of which this entry is a part, were dropped from the *redeninge* between 1187 and 1255 and were transferred to the *rentes hors renenghe*[3]. That the item *ex censu Frasena* was detached from the other Waas revenues and entered separately under the *censes de Flandre* was quite normal. It is clear that the word *census* in the *Grote Brief* of 1187 corresponded to the word *cense* in thirteenth-century documents and that its meaning in both cases was "farm." The only difference was that the *cense* of Vrasene in 1296 was a fixed-term lease, while that of 1187 may have been a fee-farm.

To support the assertion that *census* in the *Grote Brief* of 1187 meant "farm" let us cite some characteristic examples[4]. Most receipts *ex censu* consisted of money, though there were some farm-rents in kind, as is seen in the account of Bapaume where there were certain quantities of wheat and oats *ex censu* and receipts *ex terragiis*[5]. It should be noticed that the receipts *ex censu* often in round figures either represented most of the money received from a circumscription (for example Aire: 40 *l.* from a total of 87 *l.;* Harelbeke: 47 *l.* from a total of 47 *l.;* Bruges-*brevia* de Roia: 215 *l.* from a total of 382 *l.*)[6] or all of it, as was the case at Locres, Houtem, and Aalter, centers which may have been established to collect the farms[7]. The item "In nummis ex censu Lilerii cervisie, anserum, trabonum, caponum 105 *l.*

---

[1] Algemeen Rijksarchief at Brussels, Rekenkamer, *Rolrekeningen*, no. 266 (*renenghelle* of 1296).

[2] Verhulst and Gysseling, *Compte général*, pp. 145, 68-69.

[3] They no longer appear on the *Grote Brief* of 1255.

[4] Verhulst and Gysseling, *Compte général*, p. 197.

[5] *Ibid.*, p. 159.

[6] *Ibid.*, pp. 155, 170-171.

[7] *Ibid.*, pp. 190-192, 145, 89, 98.

16 *s.* preter 1 obolum" in the account of Lillers may be interpreted to mean that the domanial rents consisting of beer, geese, bustards, and capons were farmed as a whole for a fixed rent[1]. While the receipts of wheat and oats *ex redditibus* (domanial rents) were entered separately *(ex redditibus tritici 17 ¹/₂ boisteaus. . . avene ex redditibus 3 m° 4 vasa)*, this was not the case for beer, geese, and the like, which consequently must have been farmed out as a whole. Unfortunately it is only for Lillers that we have a detailed description of the farm. Consequently we cannot say what revenues were farmed out and entered as a single item *ex censu* in the *Grote Brief*. Probably they consisted of domanial rents of various kinds, and this would explain why the entry *ex censu* does not appear with revenues from a single right such as tolls, mints, justice, and tithes farmed out and collected in round figures where the phrase *ex censu* was obviously considered superfluous[2].

To buttress this argument we may cite a charter of Count Baldwin IX from about 1201. To the priest of the chapel in his castle at Ghent the count granted, among other revenues, "de decima de Borst, quam Rodolfus notarius sub censu tenet hereditario 4 libre."[3] Reference to this rent in the *Grote Brief* of 1187 is found in the account of the *spicarium* of Aalst:"ex Burst pro decima 4 *l.* hoc anno."[4] From this evidence we can infer that in 1187 a person, perhaps Rodulfus, held the tithe of Burst in fee-farm for a payment of 4 *l.* Even though the *Grote Brief* does not list this receipt as *ex censu* we may conclude that by 1187 a large number of the count's revenues were farmed out. This means that their collection on the local level was entrusted to men, mostly officials of the count though some may have been private persons, who kept the real produce of the count's domain for themselves and in exchange paid to the receiver of the circumscription a yearly fixed rent, generally in a round figure, of either money or kind[5].

[1] *Ibid.*, p. 161.

[2] See above, p. 32, and p. 30, n. 5.

[3] Ch. Duvivier, *Actes et documents anciens intéressant la Belgique* (Brussels, 1903), new ser., no. 149; Strubbe, *Egidius van Breedene*, no. 1.

[4] Verhulst and Gysseling, *Compte général*, p. 193.

[5] As was the farm of the toll of St.-Omer.

All revenues, however, were not farmed out. Some large manors in the south of the county were still held in demesne. Some domanial revenues were paid by local officers directly to the receivers of the *spicaria*. In Flanders the receivers of the *spicaria* and *brevia* did not farm out the revenues as did similar officers in England and Normandy. Had they done so the receivers would not have rendered detailed account of their revenues in the *Grote Brief* of 1187 as was usually done. Some receivers, however, rendered account for only one or two sums which generally represented from 80 to 100 per cent of the total receipts of their circumscriptions. An example of this was the *scaccarium* at Veurne for which the following was the only receipt entered: "Caput eius in nummis 777 *l*. 10 *s*. 8 *d*. Ex incremento 58 *s*. 5 *d*."[1] That the relatively low sum of the *incrementum* was not incorporated into the main receipt but entered separately suggests that the main receipt was a fixed sum which may be considered a farm-rent. This reminds us of the practice in the Norman rolls where the *incrementa* of the farm, like the revenues *extra firmam*, were listed separately instead of being incorporated into the main receipt[2].

The accounts of the *spicarium* and the *census* of Courtrai are more informative. The total income of the *spicarium* consisted of oats comprised of only two sums: "Caput eius avene 1600 h. preter 1 h. Ex ministerio Hugonis notarii avene 2000 preter 14 h."[3] Here the *caput avene*, a round figure, was the product of the farm-rent. It is significant that the only receipt of the *census* at Courtrai in 1187 was 30 *l*. because in 1255 it was farmed out for a fixed rent of 60 *l*. which was just double the amount of 1187[4].

In the account of the *lardarium* of Courtrai all the various products are listed; this makes it difficult to suppose that the receipt of the *lardarium* was farmed as a whole.[5] This practice may be accounted for by the ancient origin of the account. At

[1] Verhulst and Gysseling, *Compte général*, p. 183.

[2] See below, p. 49.

[3] Verhulst and Gysseling, *Compte général*, p. 174.

[4] *Ibid.*, pp. 174-175; Luykx, *Grafelijke Financiële Bestuursinstellingen*, pp. 38-39.

[5] Verhulst and Gysseling, *Compte général*, pp. 173-174.

34

some time oats and money were taken from the *lardarium* to form receipts farmed at two separate rent-collecting centers. Apparently this was also the case with the receipts of Harelbeke (*brevia* and *spicarium*), Deinze, Coudescure, Hazebrouck, Watou, Roeselare, and Diksmuide (*spicarium*) where the receivers farmed out all the revenues. In those rent-collecting centers with revenues of a diverse nature the receivers farmed out only that part of the revenues appearing under the rubric *caput eius* which always listed receipts from a given product[1]. In such cases the *caput* represented the total of each product received without indicating its origin.

There were, then, three principal methods for the collection of the comital revenue in 1187. First, in some circumscriptions all the revenues were farmed by the receivers. Either these circumscriptions were generally small with a large manor as the center or only one kind of revenue was received from them. Secondly, there were circumscriptions where the receivers merely farmed the *caput* of a series of products and collected, besides, the revenues not incorporated in the farm. These circumscriptions were in the majority in 1187. Lastly, there were circumscriptions in which the receivers did not farm out any of the revenues.

We now have answers for some problems hitherto unsolved. We now know from which cash sums receivers had to pay the *augmentum denariorum* for which they were indebted as a supplement for part or all of their receipts when the *nummi fortes* were converted into current *denarii*[2]. We know further from which cash receipts some receivers made payments to the counts over and above their revenues and for which they were reimbursed[3]. If these receivers were farmers of the comital revenues, then the difference between the real product of the revenues farmed and the total of the farm-rent constituted their profit and a reserve from which they could make payments.

---

[1] *Ibid.*, p. 47. There are examples in the accounts of St.-Winoksbergen (*spicarium*), Diksmuide (*census*), Bruges (*spicarium*), Bruges (*brevia de Roya*), Veurne (*spicarium*), etc.

[2] *Ibid.*, pp. 64-65.

[3] *Ibid.*, p. 60.

4. *The Comital System of Accounting*

The *Grote Brief* of 1187, our only source of knowledge on the accounting system, is composed of accounts of the more than forty receivers of the circumscriptions comprising the comital domain. It was these receivers and not their subordinates who rendered account yearly at the *redeninge*. We cannot say when this accounting began, but as early as the late eleventh century some circumscriptions were considered fiscal units[1]. In this early organization the annual income from each fiscal unit was not fixed or known in advance, as was the case for most *prévôtés* and *vicomtés* in Normandy and the French royal domain. Only in a few circumscriptions were the revenues farmed as a whole. In most circumscriptions the total of the receipts was made up from all the revenues listed item by item. The order of the products, though not fixed, generally was wheat, oats, and eventually other cereals; animal products (cows, lambs, chickens); dairy products (cheese, butter, eggs); and money-rents, with the total for each revenue entered separately. This total was arrived at in the following manner. First came the *caput* of the main income which often can be identified with the farm-rent of the receiver of the circumscription. Then followed the receipts of this income not incorporated into the farm or which were an increment over it. Finally came the direct revenues of this income paid by subordinate officers or farming agents who, though rarely named, are listed as *precones, villici,* and *ministri*.

The receipts are followed by separate entries for the expenditures, also grouped income by income. The sum of the expenditures of a given income preceded the balance, which in most cases was immediately converted into money. This method facilitated the computation of the total balance for all the incomes. Consequently the next payment due to the count by the receiver of a circumscription was nearly always a sum of money.

It is clear from the preceding that, despite final conversion into money, the calculation of receipts and expenditures product by product was of fundamental importance. This archaic custom still in force as late as 1187, while suggesting the origin of the

[1] See above, p. 24.

36

system, does not allow us to say more than that the systematic conversion of receipts and expenditures in kind into money was of recent origin. There are cases still in 1187 where the next payment due by the receiver had to be made in kind, either from supplies collected during the year or those stored in the *spicarium*. In other cases only part of the balance of a product was converted into money while the other part was stored[1].

Charters by which the counts granted annual incomes from certain circumscriptions to churches show that until the second quarter of the twelfth century these incomes were generally in kind, such as cheese and herring[2]. By the end of the twelfth century, however, most incomes so assigned were in money. Only at this point were auditing sessions, such as the *redeninge*, technically possible. It is significant that this development coincided with the generalization of the *notarii* as receivers and with the separation of the treasury from the *camera* under the direction of *notarii*. Despite this conversion of incomes in kind to money on the central level it must be remembered that locally incomes were collected product by product and not converted. In 1161, for example, the rents from the inhabitants of the newly founded village of Woesten, northwest of Ypres, had to be paid in kind at Ypres, each product at a different term[3]. In 1187 it was only in one or two circumscriptions that receipts in kind were converted into money at the local level[4]. Not until the fourteenth century was a topographical order substituted for the old system of product by product[5].

Previously it was suggested that until the middle of the twelfth century there was no central auditing system but that auditing occurred only locally for the circumscription. This conclusion rested upon the existence of local assemblies (known as *redeninge* summoned and presided over by the provost-chancellor between 1167 and 1178) of the count's receiver at Veurne[6]. The profits from the cutting of the tallies received by the provost-chancellor

---

[1] Verhulst and Gysseling, *Compte général*, pp. 55-57.
[2] *Ibid.*, pp. 135-137.
[3] See the charter cited on p. 22, n. 2.
[4] Verhulst and Gysseling, *Compte général*, p. 55.
[5] Monier, *Institutions financières*, p. 44.
[6] See above, p. 28.

in the thirteenth century probably derived from the twelfth-century *redeninge* at Veurne and at St.-Winoksbergen[1].

Over these local *redeninge* was established during the second half of the twelfth century a central auditing meeting of the *ratiocinatores supremi*. The *Grote Brief* of 1187 indicates that this session was held in early June; later and during the whole thirteenth century it was held on 24 June (Nativity of St. John the Baptist)[2]. This session was held when the payments from receivers of the *spicaria* were due. In reality the payments of the receivers were due at the treasury three times a year: within the week following St. Martin's Day (11 November), on Candlemas (2 February), and on Ascension Day[3], but the final audit at the *redeninge* was only held after the three payments had been made and as soon as possible after Ascension Day[4]. It follows therefore that the *redeninge* was concerned only with the audit of accounts. During the *redeninge* only the net debt remaining after the third payment on Ascension Day was probably cleared off. In the *Grote Brief* of 1187 the entry *inde datum comiti cum vadiis* consequently refers to payments into the treasury made prior to the *redeninge*. The entries *debet adhuc* or *remanet sub eo* represent the debt remaining which was completely or partly settled at the *redeninge*, or sometimes not settled at all[5]. Where

[1] See p. 17, n. 3 and p. 28, n. 1.

[2] See above p. 27, n. 2.

[3] Charter of Count Baldwin IX, dated 1195-1199, to his chapel at Courtrai: "Hec autem XLVI lb. . . solventur eis tribus terminis anni, sicut michi solventur redditus mei; . . . tercia pars infra octavam sancti Martini; altera tercia pars infra octavam Purificationis beate Marie; ultima tercia pars infra octavam Ascentionis Domini" (Miraeus-Foppens, *Opera Diplomatica*, IV, no. LIV). For other references to dates of the accounting see Gilliodts-Van Severen, *Coutume de la prévôté de Bruges*, I, 17-18; Luykx, *Grafelijke Financiële Bestuursinstellingen*, no. 125.

[4] See the passage in Galbert de Bruges cited in n. 2, p. 16. It was on Ascension Day that the *berquarii* and *custodes curtium* came to make their payments to the count. That they did this without receipt of an order indicates that Ascension Day was a date established by custom. It should be noted that the account published by Strubbe, *Fragment*, extends from 13 November 1140 to 24 January 1141 and is concerned with the period between St. Martin's and Candlemas. Strubbe (pp. 18-19) is therefore wrong to argue that the annual audit of the accounts occurred in November.

[5] This revises the statements of Verhulst and Gysseling, *Compte général*, pp. 58-60.

receivers had paid their total net debt before the *redeninge*, their account ended simply with the notation *quod totum solvit*[1].

Information on auditing the accounts of the receivers of the *spicaria* and *brevia* at the *redeninge* is lacking. Probably the accounts of preceding years and other written documents enabled verification of the farms and other revenues. Tallies served as vouchers for payments made into the treasury at the three times of payment[2]. The *redeninge* was a meeting where all present were able to observe and give their approbation to the calculations connected with the auditing. This was achieved by the use of counters moved about on a table covered with a cloth lined into columns, a system which employed the principles of the abacus[3]. The word *scaccarium* by which this system was known is found for the first time in Flanders at the beginning of the thirteenth century to describe the local *redeninge* sessions of the *brevia* at Veurne and the *magna brevia* at Bruges[4]. Because these were centers for the collection of revenue in money it was natural to use the system of the abacus. At the annual general *redeninge* where all receipts and expenditures including those in kind were converted into money we can suppose that this implied the use of the *scaccarium* even though it was not so called. It should be remembered that the auditing body of Normandy long bore the name *curia* before being called *scaccarium*. It is logical to assume, therefore, that the *scaccarium* system of accounting was used in twelfth-century Flanders because by the first half of the century the principles of the abacus were well known[5].

The notary Galbert of Bruges tells us that in 1127 two members of the chapter of St. Donatian at Bruges, undoubtedly clerks of the count's chancery, were studying at the cathedral

---

[1] For a more detailed discussion of this problem see Verhulst and Gysseling, *Compte général*, p. 44.

[2] See Strubbe, *Fragment*, and p. 17 above.

[3] See the similar conclusions on the English exchequer by H. G. Richardson and G. O. Sayles, *The Governance of Mediaeval England* (Edinburgh, 1963), p. 260.

[4] Verhulst and Gysseling, *Compte général*, pp. 60, 83.

[5] L. Delisle, "Des revenus publics en Normandie au douzième siècle," *Bibliothèque de l'École des Chartes*, V (1848-1849), 271. See also Perroy, in *Revue du Nord*, XLIV (1962), 445.

school of Laon, famous for study of mathematics and the abacus[1]. Perhaps, as has been suggested, the English exchequer derived its knowledge of the abacus from Laon[2]. It is possible that the two clerks from St. Donatian learned the technique of the abacus at Laon and brought this knowledge back to Bruges where it eventually was used for the auditing of accounts.

[1] Galbert de Bruges, Ch. XII, p. 22.
[2] See the discussion below, pp. 67-68.

CHAPTER III

A COMPARISON OF FLEMISH, NORMAN, AND FRENCH ROYAL FINANCIAL INSTITUTIONS FROM THE ELEVENTH TO THE THIRTEENTH CENTURY

In many respects the central organs of Flemish financial administration were similar to those of Normandy and the French royal domain. In the three states there was a distinction between the treasury and the financial administration of the princely domain. While in Flanders there was a difference between the *camera-thesaurus* and the auditing-office of the provost-chancellor, in France there was a difference between the Temple (treasury) and the *curia* which audited the royal accounts[1]. The treasurer of the Order of the Knights Templars in Paris served also as the *thesaurarius regis* but he had no role in financial administration or in the auditing of accounts which were both functions of the *curia regis*. The treasurer of the Knights Templars simply received, stored, and paid out money[2]. In the duchy of Normandy there was a similar distinction. Financial administration and collection of domanial revenues was the responsibility of the *scaccarium* headed by the seneschal which was a part of the ducal *curia*. On the other hand, the treasury headed by a treasurer had developed from the ducal *camera* and was solely concerned with the receipt, storage, and payment of money[3].

The development of central financial administration with the

---

[1] Borrelli de Serres, *Recherches sur divers services publics du XIIIe au XVIIe siècle* (Paris, 1895), I, 244-245, 299-303.

[2] *Ibid.*, pp. 237, 244, 299.

[3] Delisle, in *Biblio. de l'École des Chartes*, V (1848-1849), 268-274, 278-280; Haskins, *Norman Institutions*, pp. 175-183, 40-41, 51, 107-108, 110, 181; J. Boussard, *Le gouvernement d'Henri II Plantegenêt* (Paris, 1956), pp. 309-310.

splitting off of the treasury from the *camera* was similar in the three states. The treasury separated itself from the *camera* first in Normandy where before William the Conqueror there was a distinction between the extraordinary and occasional revenues administered by the *camera* and regular revenues from the ducal domain under the competence of the treasurer[1]. In the French royal domain during the reign of Philip Augustus a distinction was made between the treasury administered by the Temple and the *caisse de la cour* (later the *caisse de l'hôtel*) headed by the chamberlains[2]. In Flanders *camera* and treasury were combined up to the middle of the twelfth century, although during the first half of the century the eventual separation is seen in the existence of two officials, a *camerarius* and a *notarius* who operated this department. After the middle of the twelfth century the *notarius* developed his own department, the treasury, and the *camera* became a privy purse for the expenses of the count's household[3]. In the three states the treasury, after its separation from the *camera*, was entrusted to a cleric who was a specialized financial officer.

Originally the central administration and supervision of the domain in the three states rested with the *curia* which held it until the thirteenth century, but in the specialized form of the *scaccarium* in Normandy, the *curia in compotis* in the French royal domain, and the *redeninge* in Flanders. While the *curia* exercised this general financial supervision only several times a year, routine administration was entrusted, at least in Normandy and Flanders, to a member of the *curia* who, on behalf of the ruler, presided over the meetings of the *curia* devoted to auditing of accounts[4]. In Normandy the seneschal held this function; in Flanders it was the provost of the chapter of St. Donatian; in the French royal domain the officer is unknown[5].

[1] Haskins, *Norman Institutions*, p. 41; Delisle, in *Biblio. de l'École des Chartes*, V (1848-1849), 279.

[2] Borrelli de Serres, *Recherches*, I, 243, 246, 279.

[3] See above, pp. 16-19.

[4] F. Lot and R. Fawtier, *Le premier budget de la monarchie française. Le compte général de 1202-1203* (Paris, 1932), pp. 5-7; Borrelli de Serres, *Recherches*, I, 288, 302.

[5] Haskins, *Norman Institutions*, p. 180; Ganshof, in *Institutions françaises*, I, 381; Borrelli de Serres, *Recherches*, I, 300-302.

In all three states, therefore, the development of central financial administration was similar, a circumstance that may be attributed to a common origin of the institutions of these states in the Carolingian Empire[1].

From the eleventh to the thirteenth centuries collection of revenues in these three states was a part of local administration. Officers with a general competence had also local responsibilities. There is no trace of specialized financial agents, except for those collecting profits from certain princely rights, such as tolls and mints[2]. The principal local officer in Normandy, Anjou, and the French royal domain from the second quarter of the eleventh century was the *prepositus*[3]. There were other officers similar to the *prepositus* but with different names such as the *vicecomes* in Normandy, who acted as a domanial agent from the time of William the Conqueror and Henry I. Both *prepositus* and *vicecomes* had their own circumscriptions with identical functions[4]. In Flanders such an officer was called *scultetus, vicecomes, preco, minister, villicus,* or *prepositus* and his functions were identical to those of the Norman *prepositus* or *vicecomes*[5]. The difference in names may be explained by rank, principal function, or geographical location. *Preco, minister, villicus,* and *pre-*

[1] Ganshof, *La Belgique Carolingienne* (Brussels, 1958), pp. 48, 79. Although Richardson and Sayles (*Governance of Mediaeval England*, p. 245) reject the possibility of Carolingian influence on the English exchequer, they do not deny Carolingian influence on the Norman exchequer.

[2] Boussard, *Gouvernement d'Henri II*, p. 310: "l'administration financière, en ce qui concerne la perception des revenus ducaux, se confond avec l'administration intérieure du duché." Cf. Haskins, *Norman Institutions*, p. 45.

[3] For Normandy see Delisle, in *Biblio. de l'École des Chartes*, V (1848-1849), 263; Haskins, *Norman Institutions*, pp. 41-44; Boussard, *Gouvernement d'Henri II*, pp. 319-338. For Anjou see L. Halphen, *Le comté d'Anjou au XIᵉ siècle* (Paris, 1906), pp. 107-109; Boussard, *Le comté d'Anjou sous Henri Plantegenêt et ses fils (1151-1204)* (Paris, 1938), pp. 131-150; J. Chartrou, *L'Anjou de 1109 à 1151* (Paris, 1928), pp. 113-121. For the French royal domain see H. Gravier, "Essai sur les prévôts royaux," *Nouvelle Revue Historique de Droit Français et Étranger* (1903), pp. 539-574, 648-672, 806-874; W. M. Newman, *Le domaine royal sous les premiers Capétiens (987-1180)* (Paris, 1937), pp. 61-64.

[4] Delisle, in *Biblio. de l'École des Chartes*, V (1848-1849), 264; I (1849-1850), 402; Haskins, *Norman Institutions*, pp. 46-47; Boussard, *Le gouvernement d'Henri II*, pp. 323-333.

[5] Ganshof, in *Institutions françaises*, I, 402.

positus, for example, were concerned chiefly with domanial functions, but the *scultetus* or *vicecomes* had broader responsibilities and higher rank. The word *prepositus* occurs mainly in the south of Flanders and is found only as far north as Ypres and Harelbeke[1].

In Normandy and the French royal domain the *vicecomes* and *prepositus* had no superior financial officer and until the end of the twelfth century rendered their accounts directly to the central administration[2]. In Flanders this was the case only for some local agents, such as the *prepositus* and *preco;* generally such local officers were under the superior financial direction of the *notarius* who was responsible for a large circumscription. This specialization and centralization in Flanders in the late eleventh and early twelfth centuries was unique and is not found in Normandy or the French royal domain until later in the twelfth century, and then it can be traced only in Normandy. During the twelfth century the *prévôts* and *vicomtes* disappeared and their functions were farmed out to other men[3]. A similar development occurred in some *prévôtés* of the French royal domain[4]. For the first time rulers were attempting to separate fiscal from general administrative and judicial functions[5]. At this point we meet a new official, the bailiff, who arose in Normandy at the middle of the twelfth century and in the French royal domain at the end of that century[6]. Gradually as the dukes of Normandy and kings of France reorganized their *vicomtés* and *prévôtés* into larger circumscriptions known as *bailliages*, the responsibilities of the bailiffs were increased to include the collection and payment of extraordinary and variable revenues[7].

---

[1] Verhulst and Gysseling, *Compte général*, pp. 103-106; Koch, *Rechterlijke Organisatie*, pp. 85-86, 98-103, 143.

[2] Stapleton, *Magni Rotuli Scaccarii Normanniae*, vol. I; Lot and Fawtier, *Le premier budget*.

[3] Boussard, *Gouvernement d'Henri II*, pp. 333-335.

[4] Borrelli de Serres, *Recherches*, I, 14; Gravier, in *Nouv. Rev. Hist. de Droit* (1903), p. 553.

[5] Boussard, *Gouvernement d'Henri II*, p. 331.

[6] Haskins, *Norman Institutions*, p. 186; Boussard, *Gouvernement d'Henri II*, pp. 335-336; Borrelli de Serres, *Recherches*, I, 14-15, 200, 204-205; Lot and Fawtier, *Le premier budget*, p. 22.

[7] Delisle, in *Biblio. de l'École des Chartes*, V (1848-1849), 259-260; Stapleton,

The bailiffs arose in Flanders at the same time or earlier and for the same administrative reasons[1]. As in Normandy and the French royal domain the bailiff increased his financial competence. Sometimes the receivers of the *spicaria* and *brevia* became the bailiffs.

In each of the three states exploitation of the princely domain and the accounting-systems can be studied thanks to the existence of certain general accounts: in Normandy the so-called *Magni Rotuli Scaccarii Normanniae* preserved for 1180, 1195, and 1198 in whole and for 1184 and 1203 in part; in the French royal domain the account of the *prévôtés*, *bailliages*, and *marches* preserved from 1 November 1202 to May 1203; in Flanders the *Grote Brief* of 1187. Each of these accounts is the oldest known and points to a centralization of finance occurring about the same time in each state.

The *Magni Rotuli* of Normandy were records established for the annual auditing of the *scaccarium* at Michaelmas, just as was the *Grote Brief* of Flanders for the *redeninge*[2]. The general account of the French royal domain had a similar function[3]. Though identical in function, the three accounts contained different information. The *Magni Rotuli*, which were the most comprehensive, listed most of the ducal receipts (manorial and judicial) and expenditures and embraced the accounts of the older local officers *(vicomtes* and *prévôts)* and of the bailiffs[4]. The financial information in the *Grote Brief* of Flanders was

Magni Rotuli Scaccarii Normanniae, I, xxxiii-xxxiv; Haskins, *Norman Institutions*, p. 151.

[1] Nowé, *Baillis comtaux*, pp. 17-22.

[2] Delisle, in *Biblio. de l'École des Chartes*, V (1848-1849), 274-276.

[3] Lot and Fawtier, *Le premier budget*, p. 5; Borrelli de Serres, *Recherches*, I, 12-18, 224-225, 301-302.

[4] Despite the comprehensive nature of the Norman accounts Delisle did not consider them a complete account of the ducal receipts and expenditures: "[les grands rôles] n'embrassent d'une manière rigoureuse que les produits du domaine. Ce n'est que d'une manière accidentelle que les comptes des autres revenus y sont inscrits. Ainsi on n'y porte pas les bénéfices de l'atelier monétaire, ni de la chancellerie, ni de beaucoup de fins considérables dont le montant se versait directement dans les mains du roi . . . Nos grands rôles sont encore bien plus incomplets pour les dépenses: on n'y trouve que les sommes payées par les débiteurs de la couronne, en déduction de leur dette" (*Biblio. de l'École des Chartes*, V, 1848-1849, 277-278).

more restricted. Only those revenues collected on a territorial basis by the receivers of the *spicaria* and *brevia* were included. As in Normandy these revenues derived exclusively from the princely domain which, interpreted in the broad sense of L. Delisle and W. M. Newman, included the varied complex of comital rights[1]. In the *Grote Brief* are thus entered receipts from tolls and judicial profits, but not from all. The accounts of the bailiffs, which first appeared in 1255, were never incorporated in the *Grote Brief*[2]. As with the expenditures in the *Magni Rotuli* only those payments made by the receivers in deduction of their debts were entered in the *Grote Brief*.

According to F. Lot the general account of 1202-1203 embraced all the revenues of the French king. Lot, however, did not prove this thesis; he advanced it *a priori* on the basis of two extraordinary entries concerning military expenses of Philip Augustus. Lot, in arguing further that all the royal *prévôtés* and *bailliages* were included in this account, assumed that because the headings of these circumscriptions appeared, then all the royal receipts and expenditures were listed[3]. But this argument ignores the existence of the separate special accounts noted by Borrelli de Serres who has stated: "Les plus anciens concernent des approvisionnements de vins, blé, farines, avoines en 1227; avec quelques autres un peu postérieurs ils montrent toute une organisation de magasins fonctionnant dans chaque centre important de production, analogue à celle qui s'occupait des deniers, présentant la situation de ses denrées en existant, recettes par redevances, achats, récoltes, dépenses pour rentes concédées, dons, aumônes, livraisons aux princes, aux troupes . . ."[4] Without having seen these special accounts we cannot say what relation there was between them and the accounts of the *prévôtés* and *bailliages*, but from the description of Borrelli de Serres we have the impression that in addition to the accounts of the *prévôtés* and *bailliages*, concerned only with receipts and expenditures of money, there were other accounts for a system that administered

---

[1] Newman, *Domaine royal*, pp. 1-5; Ganshof, in *Institutions françaises*, I, 421.

[2] Nowé, *Baillis comtaux*, pp. 181-204.

[3] Lot and Fawtier, *Le premier budget*, pp. 51-54.

[4] Borrelli de Serres, *Recherches*, I, 39.

46

receipts and expenditures in kind. This system would seem to offer analogies to that of the *spicaria* in Flanders.

The three accounts of Normandy, Flanders, and the French royal domain had the form of a roll[1]. Like the English Pipe Rolls, the *Magni Rotuli* were composed of membranes stitched together at the top with the text appearing on both sides; the whole, when stored, was put into a roll[2]. The *Grote Brief*, however, was composed of membranes stitched together end to end to form a single long roll with the text continuing on the verso[3]. The French account of 1202-1203, the original of which is lost, must have been arranged in the same way[4]. In the three rolls each account of a receiver forms a separate heading. In the Flemish and French rolls these headings are clearly indicated with the name of the circumscription or its receiver written in capital letters above each heading. The *Magni Rotuli*, on the other hand, have only, at the foot of the verso side of each roll, the names of the principal financial officers whose accounts are listed in that roll[5].

The accounts of the *Magni Rotuli* are usually arranged geographically, and sometimes the name of the *bailliage* appears in capital letters at the head of the accounts of that *bailliage* listed without any perceivable order. In the account of the French royal domain each roll for the three terms has a heading in capital letters preceding the accounts of the *prepositurae*, the *servientes*, the *bailliae*, and the *marchiae*. In the *Grote Brief* the arrangements of the accounts is determined by the date of their audit at the *redeninge*. The date of audit was put at the beginning of the first account audited, and the other accounts audited the same day follow immediately but are not dated. Of the three general accounts the *Grote Brief*, therefore, is the only one to give a clear idea of the chronology of the auditing[6].

---

[1] This French account was preserved thanks to the edition of N. Brussel, *Nouvel examen de l'usage général des fiefs en France* (Paris, 1750), II, cxxxix-ccx.

[2] Stapleton, *Magni Rotuli Scaccarii Normanniae*, I, ix.

[3] Verhulst and Gysseling, *Compte général*, pp. 12-17.

[4] Lot and Fawtier, *Le premier budget*, p. 3.

[5] Haskins, *Norman Institutions*, p. 177; Stapleton, *Magni Rotuli Scaccarii Normanniae*, I, ix.

[6] Verhulst and Gysseling, *Compte général*, pp. 26-34.

In all three rolls the revenues of the receivers are so arranged as to indicate their source. In the Norman and French rolls the farms of the circumscriptions always appear first. Because the farm was usually rendered in money there followed immediately the expenses which the receiver was allowed to deduct from his farm. When the receipts consisted of incomes other than money, the incomes were listed separately and their total amount placed at the end.

Although there are striking similarities in these three accounts their structure is determined by the way in which the finances of each state were administered. Let us now turn to the relationship between the structure of the accounts and the administration of the domain. We note first in all the accounts the final conversion of all receipts, expenses, balances, and unsettled debts into money. It is obvious from the *Grote Brief* of 1187 that, although most revenues in kind were eventually converted into money, the counts of Flanders still received much more of their income in kind than did the dukes of Normandy and the kings of France. This suggests that financial administration in Flanders was less advanced than that in France and, especially, in Normandy.

In Normandy, although almost all incomes in kind were converted into money, many of the fixed expenses continued to be expressed in terms of kind despite the fact that they were increasingly paid in money[1]. The systematic conversion into money of the ducal revenues during the reign of Henry I coincides with the rise of the Norman exchequer which marks the reorganization of Norman finance[2]. The same connection can be made in Flanders between the rise of the *redeninge* and the increasing conversion of incomes from kind into money. Because of the paucity of evidence, especially for the French royal domain, it is rash to speculate on the tempo of economic development and financial advance in these three states. All that may be said is that Normandy was the most progressive, followed

[1] Stapleton, *Magni Rotuli Scaccarii Normanniae*, I, lix, lxv, lxxvii, lxxiv, 1, 9, 25, 30.

[2] See below, p. 51; Delisle, in *Biblio. de l'École des Chartes*, V (1848-1849), 268-274; Haskins, *Norman Institutions*, pp. 40, 45, 88, 175; Boussard, *Gouvernement d'Henri II*, p. 310.

48

closely by Flanders. That the French kings still granted rents in kind in the early thirteenth century shows a lag in the economy of the French royal domain[1].

To obtain good coin and all that was due them was a concern of the rulers of these three states. We do not know what method was used to test the quality of money in Normandy and the French royal domain. In Flanders, during the second half of the twelfth century, a system of assaying money developed at the *scaccaria* of Bruges and Veurne similar to that existing in England[2] since the early part of the century known as "money blanch."[3]

Common to the exploitation of the princely domain in these three states was the use of the farm. While it is impossible to calculate the percentage of the revenues farmed out by the rulers, one has the impression that the farm system was furthest developed in Normandy where all farms were systematically expressed in money, mostly in round figures. The French royal domain would seem also to be ahead of Flanders because all *prévôtés* were farmed out. The French system was the most simple. In the account of 1202-1203, for example, the revenues of the *prévôtés* consisted of a single farm-rent paid in three terms. Only those revenues listed under the rubric *de senescalcia* were not included in the farm[4]. The farming systems of Normandy, especially for Rouen, Caen, and Dieppe, and of Flanders were more complicated. In Normandy, rather than adding the increased revenues from a growing ducal domain to the old farms, the new revenues were listed and farmed separately under such rubrics as *de nova firma* and *de accrescenti*[5]. As can be seen

[1] Haskins, *Norman Institutions*, p. 45.

[2] Poole, *Exchequer in the Twelfth Century*, pp. 60-66; Haskins, *Norman Institutions*, p. 176; Stapleton, *Magni Rotuli Scaccarii Normanniae*, I, xvi; C. Johnson, *Dialogus de Scaccario* (London, 1950), pp. xxxviii-xli; Boussard, *Gouvernement d'Henri II*, pp. 269-272.

[3] Verhulst and Gysseling, *Compte général*, pp. 61-65. Perroy's argument that money blanch did not exist in Flanders but that a customary scale of conversion was used for the conversion of *nummi fortes* is probably correct (*Revue du Nord*, XLIV, 1962, 445).

[4] Lot and Fawtier, *Le premier budget*, pp. 4-11.

[5] Stapleton, *Magni Rotuli Scaccarii Normanniae*, I, 56, 68, 70; Haskins, *Norman Institutions*, p. 178.

from the *Grote Brief* the same procedure was followed in Flanders and new revenues were listed under the rubric *ex incremento*[1]. Likewise, when a farm was diminished it was noted by the word *imparatum* and the amount was deducted from the total debt of the receiver in that part of the account dealing with expenses[2]. These transactions were more complicated in Flanders than in Normandy because the farm rents consisted of both money and renders in kind, the receivers accounted not only for the revenues they farmed but also for those farmed out to others, and the receivers accounted for the farmed revenues as well as those collected in other ways.

Why were the *Magni Rotuli* of Normandy and the *Grote Brief* of Flanders more complicated than the French account of 1202-1203 ? The most reasonable answer is that the farming systems of Normandy and Flanders developed much earlier and were more entrenched, while that of the French royal domain, developing later, was more flexible and geared to economic change[3]. In Normandy the farm system existed as early as William the Conqueror; in Flanders it went back to the early twelfth century[4]. Unlike the situation in England, the development of the farm system on the Continent has been little studied. Its origin, however, must be found in the practice during the Carolingian period of continental abbeys demanding fixed and regular payments in kind from their manors[5]. This system was later extended to the exploitation of the *Meierhöfe* in northwest Germany and in Bavaria[6]. It is dubious, therefore, that the farm system came to the Continent from England via Normandy. What is more

[1] Verhulst and Gysseling, *Compte général*, pp. 48, 201.

[2] *Ibid.*, pp. 48, 53-54, 201. Cf. the remarks of Delisle, in *Biblio. de l'École des Chartes*, V (1848-1849), 281.

[3] Lot and Fawtier, *Le premier budget*, p. 8; Gravier, in *Nouv. Rev. Hist. de Droit* (1903), p. 550.

[4] Haskins, *Norman Institutions*, p. 43.

[5] Certainly this was true for the administration of large estates. See especially G. Duby, *L'économie rurale et la vie des campagnes dans l'Occident médiéval* (Paris, 1962), II, 391-395, 398. See also E. Lesne, *Histoire de la propriété ecclésiastique en France* (Lille, 1943), VI, 215-219.

[6] Ch.-E. Perrin, *La seigneurie rurale en France et en Allemagne du début du IXe à la fin du XIIe siècle* (Les Cours de Sorbonne, Paris, 1953), III, 1, pp. 284-296; Duby, *Economie rurale*, II, 392-393.

likely is that the farm system developed on the Continent first with its antecedents in Carolingian practices. English influence in Normandy can be seen, however, as early as William the Conqueror and Henry I in the uniform method of stipulating farms in round sums of money, a system peculiar at that moment to England and Normandy[1]. This system was adopted later in the French royal domain during the reign of Philip Augustus[2].

In Flanders where the farm system was not as generalized, only some fiscal circumscriptions were wholly farmed[3]. As we have seen, most farms even in the second half of the twelfth century were composed of incomes in kind stored in such centers as the *spicaria*, *lardaria*, and *vaccariae* which also were selected to receive revenues in money. Although centers of this type existed also for the Norman dukes and the French kings, they lost their importance in the territorial administration of finance when the farm system was uniformly introduced to all the circumscriptions[4]. In Flanders these centers preserved their importance, probably because in the late eleventh century when organized into larger fiscal circumscriptions headed by the *notarii* many were retained as administrative centers for the collection of incomes in kind and in money. This would explain why in Flanders the *spicaria*, *lardaria*, and *vaccariae* maintained an essential function in territorial finance, why the farm system was not applied to all comital revenues, and why farm revenues in kind continued to exist.

That the financial institutions of Flanders, Normandy, and the French royal domain had such striking similarities derives in part from their common Carolingian and post-Carolingian origins. In the late eleventh and twelfth centuries, although the financial institutions of these states developed along somewhat

[1] Haskins, *Norman Institutions*, pp. 42-44. R. Lennard has emphasized English influence on Norman financial administration during the reigns of William the Conqueror and Henry I (*Rural England, 1086-1135: A Study of Social and Agrarian Conditions*, London, 1959, pp. 139-140).

[2] Gravier, in *Nouv. Rev. Hist. de Droit* (1903), p. 547.

[3] These were small circumscriptions corresponding to a former *villa* or *curtis* or a place where only one type of income was collected.

[4] Delisle, in *Biblio. de l'École des Chartes*, V (1849-1850), 410; Stapleton, *Magni Rotuli Scaccarii Normanniae*, I, lxxxiii; Borrelli de Serres, *Recherches*, I, 39.

different lines and with different tempo, their basic structure was similar. Financial reorganization occurred first and most fully in Normandy under the stimulus of the English state. Thereafter Norman financial institutions resembled those of England far more than those of the Continent. Financial reorganization came later in the twelfth century in Flanders, and in the French royal domain not until the reign of Philip Augustus.

Located next to each other and facing similar political and economic demands, the financial institutions of these states could only develop along the same lines. That those of Normandy developed first was due largely to Norman administrative capacity; that those of Flanders followed closely was due to the advanced economy and to the exceptional abilities of the counts in the late eleventh and twelfth centuries; that those of the French royal domain lagged behind was due to the lack of strong rule and political stability and to economic retardation. How much institutional know-how was copied or borrowed is difficult to say, but it is obvious that the financial institutions of the French kings drew largely upon those of Normandy and probably of Flanders. In what direction the influences ran between Normandy and Flanders is more difficult to determine. If one speaks of the generalization of the farm system, the conversion of incomes from kind into money, and the administration of the exchequer, Normandy was definitely the leader. If one speaks of financial centralization under a provost-chancellor, accountability and control over financial officers like the *notarii*, and the creation of manageable fiscal circumscriptions, Flanders was the leader. To say more than this would be rash because in whatever direction the influences ran the similarity of financial development in Flanders, Normandy, and the French royal domain stemmed largely from their proximity and their common history.

CHAPTER IV

FLEMISH AND ENGLISH FINANCIAL ADMINISTRATION

1. *Early Flemish and English Financial Institutions*

In the Europe of the ninth and tenth centuries which endured the agony of renewed assaults by its enemies from north, south, and east; underwent Carolingian disintegration; and was divided by feudal reorganization into small political units, all the new states, despite the variety of institutions which emerged, owed something of their organization to Carolingian government[1]. This was particularly evident with the entourages of the princes. All the principal rulers such as the German emperors, the Capetians, the dukes of Normandy and Aquitaine, and the counts of Flanders and Anjou had their courts and their intimate households. By the eleventh century *curia regis*, *curia ducis*, and *curia comitis* are common expressions in the records. These courts were of two sizes. The large court consisted of all the great vassals of the prince who were summoned occasionally for feudal business and important affairs of state. The small court,

---

[1] L. Halphen, *Charlemagne et l'empire carolingien* (Paris, 1947), pp. 155-165; H. Fichtenau, *The Carolingian Empire* (Oxford, 1957), pp. 104-143; R. Folz, *Le souvenir et la légende de Charlemagne dans l'empire germanique* (Paris, 1949). F. Lot and R. Fawtier have written: "C'est dans le passé que les Français du moyen âge ont cherché les modèles à suivre. Les Capétiens ont conçu la royauté sous l'aspect revêtu par elle au temps de Charlemagne. . ." (*Histoire des institutions françaises au moyen âge*, Paris, 1958, II, 10). See the excellent article of F. L. Ganshof with its conclusion that "la connaissance des traits essentiels du système d'institutions de la monarchie franque est indispensable à tout effort sérieux pour comprendre la structure des états et même des grandes principautés territoriales, de l'Europe Occidentale et Centrale de la fin du IXe au début du XIIIe siècle" ("Les traits généraux du système d'institutions de la monarchie franque," *Settimane di Studio del Centro Italiano di Studi Sull' alto Medioevo*, IX, 1961, 91-127).

although duplicating most functions of the large, met more frequently and included only a few powerful and intimate vassals along with a core of administrators from the princely household[1]. Though historians still do not know to what extent Carolingian government may have influenced the Anglo-Saxon state which arose in the tenth century, and though feudalism cannot be said to have existed in England until after the Norman Conquest, we have here a royal court and household that assisted the king in the governance of his realm[2]. The historian of central institutions must fasten his eyes upon the small court or council and the household because from them emanated the principal organs of medieval government.

Recognizing that pace of institutional development differed from state to state and that local regional needs resulted in a certain amount of institutional variation, one can say that by 1200 the central institutions of England, Normandy, Flanders, and the Île de France were essentially alike. The growth and organization of central government were, however, quickest and most efficient in England and Flanders. In the England of William the Conqueror and in the Flanders of Baldwin V the households were efficiently organized and composed of a chancellor, chamberlain (in England there were several), seneschal or steward, butler, marshal, constable, and lesser functionaries like clerks and menial servants[3]. Except for the Flemish seneschal, most of these officers are unimportant because, unlike the chancellor and chamberlain, they remained so domestic or so personal in the service rendered to the prince that they never gave birth to those central institutions which assumed a dominant role in medieval government. It is to the chancellor in Flanders and the cham-

---

[1] See, for example, F. L. Ganshof, in *Institutions françaises*, I, 385-389; R. Fawtier, *Les Capétiens et la France* (Paris, 1942), pp. 163-191; Lot and Fawtier, *Institutions françaises*, II, 9-96.

[2] L. M. Larson, *The King's Household in England Before the Norman Conquest* (Madison, Wis., 1904); T. F. Tout, *Chapters in the Administrative History of Mediaeval England* (Manchester, 1937), I, 10-17; T. Oleson, *The Witenagemot in the Reign of Edward the Confessor* (Toronto, 1955).

[3] Tout, *Chapters*, I, 18-31, 67-73; G. H. White, "The Household of the Norman Kings," *Transactions of the Royal Historical Society*, XXX (1948), 127-155; F. L. Ganshof, in *Institutions françaises*, I, 378-384; R. Monier, *Les institutions centrales du comté de Flandre* (Paris, 1944), pp. 40-50.

berlains in England that one must look when tracing the rise of the efficient financial institutions which characterized both countries in the twelfth century.

Constantly attending the prince in his household when he was both sedentary and itinerant was the household staff, especially the chancellor and chamberlain. The household officers were the most important members of princely councils because their knowledge of government was professional; it was they who gave advice on technical problems unobtainable from men outside of and not in daily contact with government. They, and not the limited group of great magnates who attended meetings with a certain regularity, supplied the expert counsel and were the core of the small councils of the English and Flemish rulers. The magnates supplied a political counsel reflecting the wider sentiment of the feudal community and served as non-professional observers and supervisors of the governmental routine. Together these two bodies of councillors helped the prince to arrive at and to implement decisions. Within the small council, therefore, the household staff did most of the work while the other members supervised and busied themselves in affairs outside the routine of government. In matters of war, political questions, and justice, however, the great magnates assumed a paramount position and the household officers supplied necessary information and acted upon the decisions. What must be remembered is that the small council was actually a court or body and that the household supplied some members of the council who came to head up special departments with staffs and records. With this known it is easier to understand how the small council and household produced administrative organs to handle the finances of England and Flanders[1].

In the tenth and eleventh centuries when finally the records enable one to describe the institutions of the central government, the chamberlain emerges as a principal officer in the households

[1] In writing about the *curia regis* Tout has said: "It was quite as much a gathering of the king's *familiares*, of his household servants, as of his chief barons" (*Chapters*, I, 10-11). J. F. Baldwin has stated that the king's council was a body of men and a court which produced and maintained close ties with royal departments of government (*The King's Council*, Oxford, 1913, pp. 16-37).

of both the English kings and the Flemish counts. Known in Latin as *camerarius* or *cubicularius*, he was also called *burthegn* or *bedthegn* in Anglo-Saxon. Until the twelfth century there was probably a single chamberlain in Flanders but in England from the late tenth century to 1066 there were at least two chamberlains and sometimes three. Because the chamberlain was in charge of the princely chamber *(camera)* or appartments he not only supervised their care but took custody over all that was stored in the chamber. Whatever was precious to the prince— his clothes, jewels, or money—was kept close to him during this period of primitive government, and all that the prince had could be stored in a few chests and boxes and readily carted about the country during the habitual movement of the princely entourage. It was assumed that what was precious should be kept safe and that the safest place was close to the prince. So it was that the chamberlain, originally only concerned with the living quarters, came to have custody of his master's valuables[1].

As medieval government responded to the political and economic recovery of the eleventh century more treasure inevitably came to the prince and more had to be disbursed for increased services. To the chamberlain fell the tasks of receiving and disbursing the princely income and, as these tasks grew, those of a domestic nature became less important. Until the end of the twelfth century, both in England and Flanders, the chamberlain retained his domestic responsibilities, but inevitably his proximity to the princely treasure transformed him into an officer closely bound to the evolving institutions of central finance. In Flanders, as we have seen, during the early twelfth century there arose a central treasury located at Bruges known as the *camera* or *thesaurus*. It stored comital revenues both from domanial and non-domanial sources. In charge of this treasury was a principal chamberlain assisted by one or two other chamberlains and by a notary *(notarius)* who seems to have been responsible for the necessary records. There were other *notarii*

---

[1] Larson, *King's Household*, pp. 124, 128-133; R. L. Poole, *The Exchequer in the Twelfth Century* (Oxford, 1912), pp. 21-26; Tout, *Chapters*, I, 67-71; Ganshof, in *Institutions françaises*, I, 379-381; Monier, *Institutions centrales*, pp. 45-50.

in the area of Bruges but, as we shall observe, their functions were not intimately associated with the *camera* and the household[1].

Better informed about the English chamber in the tenth and eleventh centuries, we can say that it paralleled the work of the Flemish chamber but surpassed it in scope of operations. It is upon the scope of operations, however, that historians differ. A number of them including T. F. Tout and R. L. Poole have argued that all financial operations centered in the chamber down to the Norman period. According to this argument the chamber both stored the royal treasure and supervised its collection and disbursement[2]. Other scholars such as V. H. Galbraith and F. M. Stenton would agree that all financial direction came from the chamber but that prior to 1066 there had developed an adjunct to the chamber, the treasury at Winchester, which assumed the principal burden of storing the king's income and of keeping the chamber supplied with money. The chamber continued to receive royal income directly, as it was to do for centuries, but the treasury was a reservoir from which money could always be obtained[3]. Although a treasury probably did not exist much before the Conquest the Galbraith-Stenton position seems better supported by the evidence; at least under Canute and Edward the Confessor there was a treasury at Winchester.

Leaving for a moment the relations of chamber to treasury we see that by the middle of the eleventh century the chamber staff presided over a reasonably sophisticated financial machin-

[1] See above, pp. 12-18; Ganshof, in *Institutions françaises*, I, 380. In his account of the murder of Count Charles the Good of Flanders, Galbert of Bruges referred to Arnold the chamberlain as responsible for the treasury. He wrote: "Interim consiliabatur Isaac cum Borsiardo, quid melius faceret, utrum ibidem occideret an vitae adhuc reservaret, donec extorquerent ab eo omnem comitis thesaurum, simul et ab Arnoldo camerario quem presentem captivaverant" (H. Pirenne, *Histoire du meurtre de Charles le Bon comte de Flandre (1127-1128) par Galbert de Bruges*, Paris, 1891, Ch. XVIII, p. 32).

[2] Tout, *Chapters*, I, 73; Poole, *Exchequer*, p. 23.

[3] V. H. Galbraith, *Studies in the Public Records* (London, 1948), pp. 42-46; F. M. Stenton, *Anglo-Saxon England* (Oxford, 1943), p. 635. See also J. H. Round, "The Origin of the Exchequer," in *The Commune of London* (London, 1899), pp. 62-96.

ery. When the king and his entourage were sedentary, as at Winchester or Westminster, the chamber was located in the royal appartments. Always an essential part of the chamber was the wardrobe *(garderoba)* which was literally a small room wherein were kept the king's robes and where also the chamber staff stored the royal treasure and valuables in appropriate chests. When the royal household became itinerant the chamber staff then occupied any rooms available enroute and the wardrobe was reduced to a group of chests and boxes into which was put and from which was taken the royal income[1]. For administering solely to the financial needs of the king and his entourage such a simple organization sufficed, but by the mid-eleventh century there was need for a larger organization with machinery adequate to collect various incomes from all over the realm, to store them, to disburse some of them, and to account for them.

Besides menial servants who kept the royal quarters and clothes in order, the chief or master chamberlain was also assisted by one or two chamberlains who concerned themselves with the king's privy purse for immediate financial needs and also supervised a financial system which radiated throughout the realm[2]. Accountable to the chamber prior to 1066 were the sheriffs of the shires who were responsible for collection of the king's income. The sheriff had to render the annual farm *(feorm)* of the shire to the chamber. Originally consisting of payments in kind from the royal manors, by the eleventh century most of these renders had been converted into money. What was still rendered in kind was evaluated in money. Though the payments in money were made directly to the chamber, this was not always the case with the renders in kind. These were often stored in local granaries and storehouses of the shire and then funneled to the royal household or supplied to the king and his entourage when they were in the shire. Even before 1066 some of the revenue never got to the chamber or storehouses because it was paid by the sheriffs to various royal servants, creditors, or ecclesiastical establishments. Throughout the elev-

[1] Tout, *Chapters*, I, 67-71.
[2] Tout, *Chapters*, I, 72-74; Poole, *Exchequer*, pp. 20-26; J. H. Round, *The King's Serjeants and Officers of State* (London, 1911), p. 121.

58

enth century the farm of the shires contributed a major share of the royal income and the rest came from other revenues collected by the sheriff and his subordinates, such as judicial incomes which included fines *(wites)*, compositions, and forfeitures. After 991 the sheriff collected the Danegeld whenever it was assessed, and he was ultimately responsible for the sums owed by boroughs *(firma burgi)* and other special units of the shire[1].

At least once a year and possibly more often the sheriffs had to render account of their payments. To handle this work the chamber had by 1066 developed an efficient procedure and machinery. The farms of some shires were arranged so that all the incomes from the royal estates were paid annually in a lump sum. This entailed a strict system of accountability to insure accurate rendering of the sum. The most common method of payment was by tale *(ad numerum)* which required a strict inspection to insure that 240 d. were paid for each pound owed. A more rigorous method stipulated payment by weight *(ad pensum)* which meant that the weight of a good royal pound of 240 d. had to be balanced by the pound received. Though it is uncertain whether in the eleventh century money was paid at a fixed rate *(ad scalam)*, whereby vantage-money at the rate of 6 d. per pound was added, it is definite that payment blanch was employed. Under this system an assay was made of the money received to insure that the royal standard of coinage, the correct ratio of silver and alloy, was met. This method requiring men familiar with some chemical knowledge was later adopted by the exchequer because it was the most accurate. Whether these transactions were recorded is not known but we do know that tallies were used to reckon the accounts. These wooden records or receipts continued to be used throughout the Middle

---

[1] In his account of the farm of the shire Poole wrote: "Whether therefore cattle or wheat or silver pennies were rendered at the Treasury, they were reckoned in money" (*Exchequer*, p. 30). The fullest account of the collection of the farm of the shire is in W. A. Morris, *The Medieval English Sheriff to 1300* (Manchester, 1927), pp. 28-33. See also R. S. Hoyt, *The Royal Demesne in English Constitutional History: 1066-1272* (Ithaca, 1950), pp. 1-51; Stenton, *Anglo-Saxon England*, pp. 284-286, 476; Round, *Commune of London*, p. 72; W. Parow, *Compotus Vicecomitis* (Berlin, 1906).

Ages. A tally-cutter *(tallator)*, skilled in cutting the appropriate notches, must have been attached to the chamber[1].

During the Middle Ages the life of the English kings was itinerant, more so in the eleventh century than later when they could govern more efficiently from a fixed point. When their financial need was simple the chamber arrangement was adequate and probably more efficient because the chamber accompanied the king and provided for his food and money. Even in the eleventh century, however, this system was proving inadequate; it was impossible to store and cart about all the money and valuables in chests. It seems certain, therefore, though there is no evidence for it until the Normans, that there developed from the chamber, but still staffed by it and under its supervision, a treasury located permanently at Winchester. From Norman evidence telling of this treasury's functions we can conclude that under the later Anglo-Saxon kings it undoubtedly guarded much of the royal income, received payments, and made disbursements, especially large ones, to keep the chamber supplied.[2] Under the Normans this treasury expanded its activity until eventually it associated with the chamber to produce the exchequer.

2. *The Late Eleventh Century: A Period of Transition*

Into the late eleventh century the English and Flemish financial systems closely paralleled each other. The chambers and their staffs were responsible for the collection, storage, and disbursement of income. There were local storehouses for the produce of the comital domain and royal manors. Although these

[1] Poole, *Exchequer*, pp. 30-35; A. Hughes, C. G. Crump, C. Johnson, *Dialogus de Scaccario by Richard, Son of Nigel Treasurer of England and Bishop of London* (Oxford, 1902), pp. 28-36; Round, *Commune of London*, p. 85; *Introduction to the Study of the Pipe Rolls*, in *Publications of the Pipe Roll Society* (London, 1884), III, 60-69; F. Liebermann, *Einleitung in den Dialogus de Scaccario* (Göttingen, 1875). For the use of tallies see H. Jenkinson, "Medieval Tallies," *Archaeologia*, LXXIV (1924), 289-351.

[2] Galbraith has argued: "We must suppose a well-organized and well-staffed Treasury at Winchester for many generations before the Conquest, and there is in fact some definite evidence of a Treasury there from the time of Cnut" (*Studies in the Public Records*, p. 45).

depots were scattered about the shire and *châtellenie*, the principal ones were generally located at the borough of the sheriff and at the *château* of the *châtelain*. While in England most of the royal income had been converted into money, in Flanders conversion into money had not progressed so far. There the treasury was at Bruges where the counts centered their government, and there was as yet but one treasury—the chamber treasury. In England, however, the storage facilities of the chamber had proved inadequate, thus leading, as we have seen, to the establishment of a separate treasury at Winchester[1]. It is at this point that both in Flanders and England increased revenues and expanding government forced further innovation which was to set the course of financial administration during the twelfth century.

The essential reform in Flanders came in 1089, or possibly a few years earlier. On 31 October 1089 the future Robert II, acting on behalf of his father Robert le Frison then absent in the Holy Land, issued a charter stipulating that henceforth the provost of the chapter of St. Donatian of Bruges would be chancellor and that, in addition to guarding the comital seal and supervising the clerical staff, he would assume control of the finances. To him were to be accountable the local collectors of revenue from the comital domain[2]. Control of finance, while still remaining in the household, shifted to the chancellor whose responsibility for auditing the accounts placed him above the chamberlain who, into the thirteenth century, was relegated to

---

[1] R. Monier, *Les institutions financières du comté de Flandre du XI⁰ siècle à 1384* (Paris, 1948), pp. 7-10; Ganshof, in *Institutions françaises*, I, 419-420; Verhulst and Gysseling, *Compte général*, pp. 54-58. See also above, pp. 13-17. For the substitution of money payments in England see Hughes, Crump, Johnson, *Dialogus de Scaccario*, pp. 32-36; Poole, *Exchequer*, pp. 30-31.

[2] F. Vercauteren, *Actes des comtes de Flandre 1071-1128* (Brussels, 1938), no. 9: "Prepositum sane ejusdem ecclesie, quicumque sit, cancellarium nostrum et omnium successorum nostrorum, susceptorem etiam et exactorem de omnibus reditibus principatus Flandrie, perpetuo constituimus, eique magisterium meorum notariorum et capellanorum et omnium clericorum in curia comitis servientium, potestative, concedimus." See also Monier, *Institutions financières*, pp. 51-52; Ganshof, in *Institutions françaises*, I, 381-382; Pirenne, "La chancellerie et les notaires des comtes de Flandre avant le XIII⁰ siècle," in *Mélanges Julien Havet* (Paris, 1895), pp. 733-748. See above, pp. 12-13.

the more pedestrian duty of receiving, guarding, and disbursing money from the chamber treasury[1]. The innovation of 1089 left financial administration completely in the household but introduced a new element of control in the chancellor who checked the accounts of the local collectors[2]. Obviously the chamberlain was informed of the amounts due from the local collectors and certainly he must have closely investigated when payments were made into the chamber treasury, but essentially he had become a receiver and distributor of comital income[3].

Meanwhile in England financial innovation moved in the direction of taking the administration and responsibility from the royal chamber and placing it in the treasury. The relation between chamber and treasury was to remain intimate but the fact is that the latter was given much of the work previously done by the former. By 1066 there was a treasury at Winchester which was as yet a division of the chamber, staffed by chamber personnel and providing a permanent storehouse for an income too large to be handled by the itinerant chamber. By the reign of Henry I the treasury had severed itself from immediate control of the chamber. How long the treasury personnel were regarded as on detached duty from the chamber is impossible to say, but undoubtedly as they remained at Winchester and assumed more financial responsibilities they gradually became separated from the chamber. In any event, by the middle of Henry I's reign the treasury was *de facto* a separate organization. It still supplied money to and worked with the chamber, but its staff and procedure were distinct. Whereas after 1066 the two chamberlains who directed the treasury had been supplied by the chamber and were responsible to the master chamberlain, they now became exclusively the personnel of the treasury. Created some time before 1130 was a treasurer who assumed responsibility for the operations at Winchester and who was normally not regarded as a member of the household, receiving maintenance only when at the royal court. Under these three

---

[1] Ganshof, in *Institutions françaises*, I, 382, 393. See above, pp. 18-19.

[2] Compare the views of Vercauteren, *Actes des comtes de Flandre*, p. 2, and of Pirenne in *Mélanges Julien Havet*, p. 745.

[3] See above, pp. 16-17.

officers was a considerable staff of minor functionaries[1]. At the chamber, meanwhile, there were changes. The master chamberlain retained overall control but delegated his functions to subordinate chamberlains. The royal appartments and domestic necessities were supervised by two chamberlains serving in rotation. The financial functions, consisting primarily of supplying the royal need and paying for services rendered to the king, were fulfilled by two other chamberlains. The master chamberlain's financial authority was restricted to the chamber; he seems to have exercised no authority over the treasurer who was equal in rank[2].

At least until the reign of William the Conqueror, and probably for some years after, the chamber verified the accounts of the sheriffs and other royal debtors and kept records of the transactions. Gradually the treasury assumed this work. By the reign of Henry I the treasury had become the center of financial administration; the sheriffs rendered their accounts to the treasurer and the two chamberlains. Records were kept noting the sums due from the sheriffs and crediting them for payments made on behalf of the king. Other records enrolled royal writs authorizing payments from the treasury or by the sheriffs. That most authoritative record, Domesday Book, was kept at the treasury for easy reference. There, too, were settled financial disputes involving the royal revenue. Increasingly clerics were added to the staff to cope with the more elaborate accounts periodically audited by barons of the king's court. The Winchester treasury had indeed superseded the chamber as the center of financial administration, and in it were most of the elements found in the later exchequer[3]. As in Flanders there had evolved a more elaborate and efficient system which began to feel the need and to make provision for periodic auditing of

[1] Tout, *Chapters*, I, 74-81; Hughes, Crump, Johnson, *Dialogus de Scaccario*, pp. 18-21; Johnson, *The Course of the Exchequer by Richard, Son of Nigel* (London, 1950), pp. xxii-xxv.

[2] Tout, *Chapters*, I, 74-81; Johnson, *Course of the Exchequer*, pp. xxv-xxvii.

[3] Poole, *Exchequer*, pp. 35-38; Tout, *Chapters*, I, 82-92; Liebermann, *Einleitung in den Dialogus de Scaccario;* White, in *Trans. Roy. Hist. Soc.*, XXX (1948), 127-155, and "Financial Administration Under Henry I," *Trans. Roy. Hist. Soc.*, VIII (1925), 56-78.

the accounts. Although both systems had the same objectives, the English system was better developed and already in the process of going out of the household.

3. *The Maturation of English and Flemish Finance in the Twelfth Century*

Though financial innovation and progress continued in Flanders and England during the thirteenth and fourteenth centuries and records became more numerous, one who follows the course of English and Flemish financial history must admit that in the less complicated twelfth century can be observed two systems operating very efficiently and seeming to be about as effective as permitted by contemporary intellectual, social, economic, and political progress. Just as the twelfth century marked a sort of golden age in political achievement in both England and Flanders, so too did it in institutional development. Innovation and organization kept pace and met the demands of exceptionally able rulers. This is not to say that subsequent institutional development did not advance beyond that of the twelfth century, but never again does one feel that financial administration so satisfactorily fulfilled the needs of the prince, that it was so nicely geared to social, economic, and political realities. In the twelfth century financial institutions seemed to keep abreast of and even ahead of the demands. Later when western Europe moved rapidly away from feudal organization this was not to be the case. Both England and Flanders even in the twelfth century were sloughing off feudal institutions and mentality, and though financial institutions had to straddle feudal and non-feudal organization they were as yet able to keep up with the pace of transition. Assuredly the England of Edward I and the Flanders of Guy de Dampierre had advanced far beyond their positions in the twelfth century, and yet one cannot truly say that they equalled the institutional perfection achieved under the Angevin dynasty and the Alsatian house. Historical circumstances, particularly political and economic, so combined at the turn of the thirteenth century as to upset the nice balance between institutional need and fulfilment; seldom was such balance to be achieved again in the Middle Ages[1].

The financial reform of Flanders in the late eleventh century placed the chancellor at the head of financial administration. Henceforth the collectors for the comital domain had to submit their accounts periodically for the chancellor's audit. The chamberlain, who to this point had been supreme in finance, was subjected to the chancellor's control and relegated to receipt and disbursement of comital income. Despite the efficiency introduced by the added element of control, all financial administration remained within the household[2]. We knew that this system functioned efficiently in the first half of the twelfth century but remained ignorant of the details until they were supplied by the *Grote Brief* of 1187, the first comprehensive financial record extant for Flanders. With the aid of this document and supplementary information provided by charters and financial records of the thirteenth century we are reasonably well informed concerning the principal features of financial administration in the twelfth century.

Let us here briefly recapitulate certain facts presented by Professor Verhulst. The fiscal year ran from April to April and the accounts of the local collectors were audited a few weeks later, in the case of the accounts in the *Grote Brief* of 1187 between 1 and 9 June. Present at the auditing session were the

---

[1] During the thirteenth century both in Flanders and England the records show how finance was in disarray. Despite innovations in accounting procedures, the development of more efficient records, and financial reform, one feels that control was lost, resulting in utter disorganization. Accountable officers fell years behind in rendering their accounts. The new money revenues had not developed enough to replace satisfactorily the old incomes in kind. In both Flanders and England the increasing reliance on loans from Italian and native bankers and merchants is a sign of the painful transition from an agrarian to a money economy.

[2] See above, pp. 16-19; Verhulst and Gysseling, *Compte général*, pp. 106 ff.; Pirenne, *Histoire de Belgique*, I, 127-130, and *Mélanges Julien Havet*, pp. 733-748; Monier, *Institutions financières*, pp. 39-41; Ganshof, in *Institutions françaises*, I, 420. See also the accounts, now superseded, in E. Bacha, *Le chancelier de Flandre* (Brussels, 1897), pp. 9-10; E. Reussens, *Les chancelleries inférieures en Belgique depuis leur origine jusqu'au commencement du XIIIe siècle* (Brussels, 1896), pp. 119-123; and R. Richebé, *Essai sur le régime financier de la Flandre avant l'institution de la chambre des comptes de Lille* (Paris, 1889).

chancellor and all the principal receivers who rendered their accounts one after another. Towards the end of the twelfth century this accounting session came to be known as the *redeninge* (*redeningha* in Latin and *renenghe* in French), named after the receivers of the comital domain who were by then called *redenaars* (*ratiocinatores* in Latin and *renneurs* in French). Some evidence indicates that there were local *redeninge* consisting of the *redenaars* from a group of *ministeria*. There was, for example, such a *redeninge* at Veurne during the last half of the twelfth century. Whether local *redeninge* composed of the *notarii* or *redenaars* from a group of *ministeria* previously audited their accounts to facilitate the final *redeninge* is not definitely known but would seem likely. Whatever may have been the preliminary preparations, the principal session was held after the end of the fiscal year in April. Here the chief receivers of the *ministeria* (*ratiocinatores supremi* or *hoofdredenaars* as they were called late in the century) presented their accounts to the chancellor at the *officium de redeninga*. At times the assembled members of the *redeninge* served as a court to adjudicate financial disputes. Gradually *redeninge* came to denote the total income of the comital domain and the disbursements made from it.

Lacking any contemporary account of one of these auditing sessions we cannot say much about the procedure. Pertinent records state only that the *notarii* or *redenaars* assembled annually with the chancellor for the auditing of accounts which were then placed together on the *Grote Brief*. Obviously the chamberlain and other household officials must have been present at the meetings to serve as a check upon the chancellor. It would be strange if the counts did not delegate members of their *curia* to act in such a capacity when this was common practice in western Europe, particularly in England and Normandy. Despite the lack of evidence we can assume that such was the procedure also in Flanders.

By the second half of the century payments in kind were rare; payments of grain were but occasionally received. Cash payments, though made in the currency of Douai, Antwerp, Artois, and in other French coins, were always converted for purposes of accounting into the value of the Flemish coinage. To insure receipt of money equal in value to a good Flemish penny a ratio was worked out whereby a specified number of pennies had to be added for each 240 pennies owed. This practice resembled the *ad scalam* system used in England during the eleventh and twelfth centuries. A more rigorous check over the quality of money was gained by enforcing payment of pennies equal in percentage of pure silver to a theoretical comital standard. Because coins in circulation seldom fulfilled this standard, the receivers had to pay additional pennies for each pound owed. The rate seems to have been determined by an assay like that in England which provided for blanch payment[1].

Nothing is known about the method of calculation employed at these auditing sessions but the chancellor and his assistants at the *redeninge* may have used the chess board system of the exchequer *(scaccarium)* which came into existence in England and Normandy early in the twelfth century. This system employed the principles of the abacus whereby counters were placed according to a set plan in columns representing sums from a penny to 10,000 *l.* We do know that the depots *(brevia)* of the *ministeria* which received payments in money were also called *scaccaria*, a term appearing in charters and other records of the early thirteenth century[2]. If this system of calculation was used in Flanders it is possible that it developed as early as in England and Normandy because the abacus had been known in Lorraine and northern France since the early eleventh century. The schools of Lorraine were recognized for their knowledge of mathematics. C. H. Haskins has convincingly argued that the abacus was introduced into England from Lorraine prior to 1100 by a royal clerk Robert of Lorraine who subsequently became bishop of Hereford (1079-1095). The abacus was also known at the cathedral school of Laon where Adelard of Bath

---

[1] See above, pp. 59-60; Verhulst and Gysseling, *Compte général*, pp. 41-69, 106-121. See also H. Nowé, *Les baillis comtaux de Flandre des origines à la fin du XIVe siècle* (Brussels, 1929), pp. 30-37, 186-187.

[2] Verhulst and Gysseling, *Compte général*, p. 60: "Au début du XIIIe siècle, les *brevia* de Furnes et les *magna brevia* de Bruges où étaient centralisées la majorité des recettes en argent de la circonscription, étaient appelés *scaccarium* (schaak, échiquier)." See p. 83 for citations of twelfth- and thirteenth-century charters referring to *scacarium Furnense* and *de scako in Furnis*.

studied and taught; here soon after 1100 he wrote his famous treatise on the abacus which, according to R. L. Poole, was the means of introducing knowledge of the abacus into England and, in the form of the chess board *(scaccarium)*, was soon used to calculate the sums owed by the sheriffs to the king[1]. With Flanders so close to Lorraine and Laon and so advanced economically, so interested in trade and industry, so tied to western Europe and England by economic and political bonds, one cannot believe that the abacus was unknown there.

In what ways did the Flemish financial administration in the twelfth century resemble the English system? Since English financial institutions in the twelfth century are so much better known than the Flemish, we need only discuss those developments that afford useful comparison. Though by the early reign of Henry I a treasury had separated itself off from the chamber and superseded it as the center of financial administration, it was not to hold this new position long. Perhaps by 1109 and definitely by 1115 the treasury was already being superseded and absorbed by the exchequer which became the dominant royal financial organ of the twelfth century. This process of absorption was completed by the early reign of Henry II and the Winchester treasury was again what it had been under the last Anglo-Saxon kings—a mere storehouse[2]. Henceforth it was

---

[1] C. H. Haskins, "Adelard of Bath," *English Historical Review*, XXVI (1911), 491-498. It should be noted that Haskins questioned whether Adelard may have known Rudolph of Bruges who studied in Spain between 1130 and 1150 and who was well-known for his work on mathematics. See Poole, *Exchequer*, pp. 42-69. See also the discussion in Johnson, *Dialogus de Scaccario*, pp. xxii-xxiii, and xxxvi ff. Haskins has also noted the institutional relations and influences between England and Norman Sicily during the twelfth century and has suggested that there may be a connection between the English *scaccarium* and the Sicilian *diwan* or *duana* ("England and Sicily in the Twelfth Century," *English Historical Review*, XXVI, 1911, 433-477, 641-665). On the problem of institutional influences between Flanders, Normandy, and England see Haskins, "Quelques problèmes de l'histoire des institutions anglo-normandes," in *Extrait du Congrès du Millénaire Normand* (Rouen, 1911), pp. 1-11.

[2] See especially Poole, *Exchequer*, pp. 38-41; Tout, *Chapters*, I, 93-99; Galbraith, *Studies in the Public Records*, pp. 42-46; White, in *Trans. Roy. Hist. Soc.*, VIII (1925), 56-78; Johnson, *Dialogus de Scaccario*, pp. xxxv, xli. See also the remarkable chapter of Round on the origin of the exchequer in *Commune of London*, pp. 62-96.

merely a treasury of the exchequer system, a local treasury that facilitated storage and payment of money in the region about Winchester. In a sense the chamber was the father of the treasury and the grandfather of the exchequer, yet it was also directly responsible for the exchequer and always intimately connected with it. Throughout the twelfth century the chamber and exchequer worked closely together, so closely that scholars like H. G. Richardson and G. O. Sayles contend that financial administration remained centered in the chamber and that the exchequer, like the exchequer of Normandy and the other treasuries of the Angevins on the Continent, was but a spoke in a wheel whose axis was the chamber[1]. While this is an overstatement of the chamber's position, it emphasizes that medieval government never became impersonal; always the king was at the center and, if an able ruler, intimately concerned with the institutions by which he governed.

Literally the exchequer was an occasion twice a year at Easter and Michaelmas when all royal officers owing money to the king came to London and rendered their accounts before a group of auditors, the barons of the exchequer[2]. Examination of the exchequer work and personnel shows, however, that it was more than two annual accounting sessions; it was an institution that functioned throughout the year. The officer in charge of the exchequer was the treasurer who previously had headed the Winchester treasury. He along with the two chamberlains, also formerly of the Winchester treasury, busied themselves with royal finance throughout the year. They were assisted by a permanent staff consisting of the treasurer's scribe who was responsible for the Pipe Rolls and other records, a calculator who worked at the accounting sessions, a cutter of tallies, and

[1] H. G. Richardson and G. O. Sayles, *The Governance of Mediaeval England* (Edinburgh, 1963), pp. 227-229.

[2] This account of the exchequer is based upon the text of the *Dialogus de Scaccario* of Richard fitz Nigel printed by Johnson. Useful discussions of this text are in the introduction by Johnson and in that of Hughes, Crump, Johnson, *Dialogus de Scaccario*. See also Poole, *Exchequer*, pp. 70-149; *Introduction to Study of Pipe Rolls*, vol. III; White, *Trans. Roy. Hist. Soc.*, VIII (1925), 56-78; Liebermann, *Einleitung in den Dialogus de Scaccario;* and T. Madox, *The History and Antiquities of the Exchequer* (London, 1711).

some minor functionaries. These men worked in the Upper Exchequer where the accounting and record-keeping were done. In the Lower Exchequer (actually the treasury) where the money was received, assayed, weighed, bagged, and stored there was another staff consisting of a clerk of the treasurer, a pesour who weighed the money, a meltor who conducted the assays, four tellers, two knights who represented the chamberlains and kept a record of receipts and disbursements on tallies, and an usher. Most, but not all of these functionaries, were busy throughout the year performing tasks connected with the daily routine of an active department.

In the Upper Exchequer the treasurer, who conducted the examination of accounts at Easter and Michaelmas, was assisted by another group of men. Some great officers of the realm were always represented even if they did not always attend. The justiciar, when present, presided. In attendance also were the chancellor, at least one great magnate such as a bishop, and, from the household, the constable and marshal. A working staff of the chancellor's deputy, clerk, and scribe along with the constable's clerk and lesser servants comprised the rest of the Upper Exchequer. The officers and functionaries of the exchequer were thus drawn from three sources. The treasurer, chamberlains, and subordinates formed the permanent staff of the exchequer. The justiciar and great magnates came from the small *curia regis*. The chancellor, though also a member of the *curia regis*, actually came from the household as did the constable and marshal. A session of the exchequer was, therefore, an occasion when the *curia regis* sat in a financial capacity to audit accounts and to make decisions on royal finance requiring the issuance of various writs and documents under the great seal. It was also an occasion requiring the presence of the household and exchequer officers. Together these men formed the barons of the exchequer who, when financial disputes arose, also sat in a judicial capacity to form the High Court of Exchequer. Unlike the Flemish system of the twelfth century, the English system was not directed from the household. Though the relations between the chamber and exchequer were close, the latter was a separate department with a staff and procedure of its own.

The accounting sessions of the Upper Exchequer, contrary to those of the Flemish *redeninge*, included besides the sheriffs and treasurer, officers of the household and great magnates of the *curia regis* who provided an additional check over both sheriffs and treasurer.

Regarding the famous accounting sessions of the exchequer, which employed the abacus in the form of counters placed on a table ruled into columns representing units of money, we need only recall that this system was introduced during the first fifteen years of Henry I's reign and perfected during that of Henry II who benefited from the expert advice of his almoner Thomas Brown and of his treasurer Richard fitz Nigel, author of the famous *Dialogus de Scaccario* which describes in detail the routine of Upper and Lower Exchequer[1]. This system, it should be emphasized, was used in Normandy before 1130[2]. What is more profitable here than to describe further the method employed by the sheriffs and other royal officers for collecting and disbursing the royal income, the details of which are readily available, is to compare the English Pipe Roll and the Flemish *Grote Brief*[3]. From these records we can learn much about the collection, disbursement, accounting, and type of revenue.

4. *The Financial Records of Flanders and England*

Though there is a roll for 1130, the English Pipe Rolls appear with regularity beginning only with the reign of Henry II. From his second regnal year they continue almost unbroken for the rest of the century. They contain a record of all the revenues

---

[1] See Johnson, *Dialogus de Scaccario*, pp. xxxv-xxxviii; Haskins, *Eng. Hist. Rev.*, XXVI (1911), 433-477, 491-498, 641-665.

[2] For the Norman exchequer and its rolls see especially the introduction of Stapleton in *Magni Rotuli Scaccarii Normanniae;* S. R. Packard, *Miscellaneous Records of the Norman Exchequer, 1199-1204,* in *Smith College Studies in History* (Northampton, Mass., 1926-1927), vol. XII. See also F. M. Powicke, *The Loss of Normandy (1189-1204)* (Manchester, 1913), pp. 43 ff., 73 ff., 343-355; and M. De Bouard, "Le Duché de Normandie," in Lot and Fawtier, *Institutions françaises*, I, 27-28.

[3] For the collection and disbursement of revenue by the sheriffs see Morris, *Medieval English Sheriff*, pp. 241-273.

due from the sheriffs of all the counties and from other officers responsible for the incomes owed to the king from his lands and possessions. This type of record, which in the twelfth century was referred to as the *rotulus de thesauro* and later as the *magnus rotulus pipae*, was apparently called a pipe roll because of its form which consisted of numerous membranes. Two membranes were sewn together to form one length, averaging between three feet and four feet eight inches, with a width of about fourteen inches. These two membranes were known as a pipe, probably because when in a roll they resembled a pipe or cylinder. Such pipes were sewn together at the tops or heads and together formed a Pipe Roll. The size depended upon the number of entries. Beautifully written with exceptional precision, the Pipe Rolls were drawn up in the exchequer previous to the Michaelmas accounting session. Except for revenues and disbursements which varied annually all the regular entries were inscribed prior to the session with space left for the exact figures which were inserted after the account had been rendered[1].

There is only one *Grote Brief* for the twelfth century, that of 1187, and then not another until 1255. This record contained all the accounts of the *ministeria* pertaining to the revenues and disbursements from the comital domain. The account of 1187 originally consisted of five membranes sewn end to end. These membranes measured in length respectively, 663, 686, 672, 645, and 655 millimeters for a total length of 3.32 meters (approximately 11 feet). Their width was 24 centimeters (approximately 10 inches). Although both recto and dorso were used, the account was much smaller than the Pipe Roll of 1187. Like the Pipe Rolls, the *Grote Brief* of 1255 and other such accounts of the thirteenth century were drawn up prior to the *redeninge* with only the variable entries left to be filled in after the accounting. As far as we know the *Grote Brief* of 1255 was compiled from

---

[1] The best discussion of the Pipe Rolls is in Poole, *Exchequer*, pp. 1-3, 150-154; and *Introduction to Study of Pipe Rolls*, vol. III. Facsimiles of Pipe Rolls are in C. Johnson and H. Jenkinson, *English Court Hand* (Oxford, 1915), Pt. II, Plates IV, V, VIII, XI. Cf. J. H. Ramsay, "The Origin of the Name 'Pipe Roll'," *English Historical Review*, XXVI (1911), 329-330, 749.

accounts *(rationes* or *brevia)* and daily chronological records of expenses and disbursements submitted beforehand by the receivers of the *ministeria*. The *Grote Brief* of 1187, however, was apparently compiled after the session of 1 to 9 June and was drawn up from a rough copy or minute made during the accounting session with the help of *brevia* previously supplied by the receivers; this method seemingly prevailed in the twelfth century. What is striking is that the method of compilation was so similar to that of the Pipe Roll. Like their English counterparts, the scribes of the *redeninge* were in possession of enough current information to be able to compile most of the *Grote Brief* in advance[1].

The arrangement of the *Grote Brief* of 1187 and, we must assume, of other such accounts of the twelfth century, was efficient and logical. The accounts for each of the *ministeria* were divided into incomes and expenses. Under incomes there first appeared those in kind such as grain. Each type was entered under the word *caput* which indicated the major part of that income (80 to 90 percent) which was a fixed income known by the chancellor. Then came entries recording the collection of smaller amounts of income in kind. Appropriate notations were made indicating an increase in the income, payments of arrears, and amounts not received or impossible to collect. Next came the total of the income received followed by a breakdown of the sources for the incomes in kind[2]. After the incomes in kind came other types which will be discussed when examining the specific revenues and disbursements of the comital income.

The order for the accounts of expenses was the same as that for the incomes. If, under the incomes, wheat came first, then payment of wheat would appear first under the expenses. The expenses listed first, which were placed after the words *in domo*, were those for the depots of the *ministeria* and for the comital entourage when in residence. Next under the word *datum* came

---

[1] Verhulst and Gysseling, *Compte général*, pp. 41-47.

[2] *Ibid.*, pp. 47-48. The account of Richard for the *épier* of Bergues-Saint-Winnoc began as follows: "Ratio Riquardi Ypris (in domo comitis) feria II[a] ante (sanctorum) Marcellini et Petri. Ex eodem anno. Caput eius tritici 115 m°. Ex Banbeka 1 m°. Ex molino de Loberga 6 m°." (p. 141).

payments for tithes and alms to churches. Lastly came diverse payments introduced by the words *super, foris super,* or *foris.* With or without *super* the word *foris* designated a series of payments. *Super,* however, designated a revenue out of which payment was made, or designated the recipient of the payments. Sometimes *super* preceded entries indicating the recipient of the payment and the source. These payments were often accompanied in the margin by the words *paratum* or *imparatum* noting whether payment had been made. What remained after these payments constituted the balance of the income which was at times consumed on the spot by the staff of the receiver or by the count and his household. Occasionally there was no balance or the balance was sold for a cash income. Sometimes all the income was consumed by payments on behalf of the count. The net profit of the account of each *ministerium* was comprised of the total of the balances of all the incomes. The net profits of all the *ministeria* made up the net profit of the year[1].

With this arrangement in mind let us look at the types of incomes and expenses. A large part of the comital income in the twelfth century still came from landed possessions. Much of the comital domain had been granted out under tenurial arrangements providing rents in kind. Arable lands produced the bulk of these rents but some also came from lands employed as pasture[2]. From the lands, buildings, and houses owned in the towns the counts derived other rents and also received payments from ovens, mills, and breweries. From tenants granted waste land to be reclaimed from the sea, marsh, dunes, and forest came other rents which, by the thirteenth century, no longer appeared on the *Grote Brief;* they were collected by other officers and accounted for to another auditing body[3]. The next

[1] *Ibid.,* pp. 49-54. The following entries from the *épier* of Veurne are typical: "Super nova feoda tritici 9 m⁰ 3 1/2 h. 1/4. . . . Foris super imparatum 1339 h. 1/4. Super nova feoda 621 h. 1/4. Super villicos avene paratum 15 1/2 h. 1/3 et imparatum 69 h. 3/4. . . . Totum avene datum et insinuatum 2945 h." (p. 180).

[2] *Ibid.,* pp. 122-123. These revenues were noted as coming *ex censu, ex redditibus, ex terragiis, ex pratis, ex pastura, ex vaccaria, ex berquaria,* etc.

[3] *Ibid.,* pp. 123-124. These revenues were noted as coming *ex veteri castello in Gant, ex port, ex macello, ex halla, ex mansuris, ex curtillis,* etc. The lands reclaimed and paying rents were called *novae terrae.*

74

important incomes were those from the seignorial rights of the counts. Among such revenues were payments by agrarian communities for use of comital resources such as wood and peat; profits of justice (collected in the thirteenth century by the bailiffs); ecclesiastical revenues such as tithes and profits of advowson; tolls from markets, fairs, bridges, and roads; profits of coinage; fees from money changers; taxes on beer and wine; public payments of *fodermolt* and *balfart* due to the counts by prescriptive usage; extraordinary taxes such as a general aid; and sundry seignorial payments. In the thirteenth century almost all these seignorial revenues were dropped from the *Grote Brief* and collected by other officers. No longer classified as incomes derived from the old comital domain, they were then lumped with various other new incomes that had no connection with the old domain and were regarded as coming from the new domain, that is, from resources not associated with the old feudal-seignorial system of exploitation[1].

Expenses were classified as fixed and occasional. The fixed expenses, those paid annually and invariable, were largely tithes granted to ecclesiastical establishments, *fiefs-rentes*, and perpetual donations such as alms. Other fixed payments were salaries to comital functionaries such as the minor officials of the *ministeria*[2]. The occasional expenses, which varied and were not paid annually, included payments for extraordinary services, remuneration for horses and equipment lost by functionaries, and repair and construction costs for comital fortifications, buildings, bridges, and dikes[3].

Such was the organization of the *Grote Brief* from which we

---

[1] *Ibid.*, pp. 124-128. *Balfart* originally obliged all men of each *châtellenie* to build and repair the comital castles. It was eventually commuted to money. *Fodermolt* obliged men holding certain lands to furnish oats for the horses of the counts and their entourage. See Ganshof, in *Institutions françaises*, I, 371; E. I. Strubbe, *Het Fragment van een Grafelijke Rekening van Vlaanderen uit 1140* (Brussels, 1950); C. Verlinden, "Le balfart," *Revue d'Histoire du Droit*, XII (1933), 107-136.

[2] On pp. 130-137 of the *Compte général* Verhulst and Gysseling have given examples of fixed and annual payments.

[3] Verhulst and Gysseling, *Compte général*, pp. 128-129. The following examples are typical: *munimento turris, ad pontem reficiendum, servienti ad equum suum*, etc.

derive our knowledge of the income and expenses of the old comital domain in the twelfth century. This traditional organization began to yield, however, in the late twelfth century to a new financial administration that concerned itself increasingly with the collection of income derived from non-seignorial and non-feudal sources and that made disbursements for non-feudal services performed by paid functionaries.

Thanks to the extremely detailed account of the Pipe Rolls in the *Dialogus de Scaccario* and to the rolls themselves, it is relatively simple to describe their organization, arranged more logically than that of the *Grote Brief*[1], except for the order of counties that varied from year to year. At the top of a pipe appeared first the names of the counties with accounts on that pipe. As the accounts became larger fewer counties appeared on a pipe. There was then a space followed by the name of the county for which the account was rendered with the name of the sheriff rendering the account on the next line. Then came the words *In Thesauro* followed by a space filled in only after the sheriff had rendered all his account and after it had been definitely established what he had paid into the exchequer. When the same sheriff had rendered account of the farm of the county for previous years and still owed money, there would appear next the words *De veteri firma* followed by the sum paid for the arrears of the preceding year's farm (the old farm). Occasionally the sheriff paid arrears *de tertio anno*. If the sheriff was new and rendering account for the first time, a notation of the arrears of the old farm *(de veteri firma comitatus)* would appear at the end of the account of the farm rather than at the beginning.

After these preliminaries came the entries recording the settled or fixed payments made annually by the sheriff from the farm of the county, which were in effect allowances to the sheriff because they were deducted from the farm of the county. Requiring no royal writ, these fixed payments included alms to churches and to the Knights Templars, tithes to religious houses,

[1] For the best discussion on the arrangement of the Pipe Rolls, see Poole, *Exchequer*, pp. 150-173; and *Introduction to Study of Pipe Rolls*, III, 42-60. The above account is also based upon *Pipe Roll 34 Henry II (1187-1188)*.

sums for charity, and wages to servants and officers of the king. Under the rubric of *Terrae Datae* came lands alienated by the king from his land in the county and for whose incomes the sheriff was not responsible. If a hundred court was alienated along with such lands, the profits of justice were lost and not accountable by the sheriff. Next followed casual payments, those not annual and fixed, which required authorization by the king's writ. Especially interesting, these entries provide details on the royal itinerary, purchases, gifts, friends, guests, construction of buildings, and other sundry matters. Finally came payments for the administration of royal justice which were authorized simply by custom of the exchequer although they varied from year to year. These were payments for executing sentences, for conducting ordeals, and for the expenses of approvers *(probatores)* who had turned king's evidence or who had acted as champions in trial by battle. Lumped with these payments were those allowed to the sheriff for transportation costs in connection with royal business. When these casual and fixed payments had been settled, the principal farm or account of the county *(corpus comitatus)* was finished.

The second and larger part of the sheriff's account dealt with payments owed to the exchequer. Whereas under the farm of the county the entries were payments out of the farm by the sheriff and were deductible from the total annual farm, the sums next listed had to be collected and turned in to the exchequer. First were the sums owed for purprestures, the encroachments made by persons upon royal land for which rents had been assessed by the itinerant justices. With these sums were payments for assarts and clearings made on royal waste and wood land. Next came the incomes from lands escheated to the crown together with payments for such feudal incidents as wardship and relief and the arrears of scutage. Then came a long list of entries concerned with judicial profits called *placita et conventiones* (pleas and agreements). Persons convicted of offenses in a royal court were placed at the king's mercy and were fined or amerced; after paying the fines they were accepted back into the royal grace. The agreements were sums paid by men to the king as a result of a settlement whereby the king promised certain advantages such as royal wardships, marriages, and escheated lands. Following this long list of entries were the taxes collected in the county, including such well-known taxes as the Danegeld, *donum*, aid, and tallage. After the taxes came the *murdrum* fines collected from the hundreds. Following each of the entries on the taxes and fines was a notation as to whether the sum had been completely paid, whether all or part of it was still owed, or why the sheriff did not have to collect and pay the full amount.

The final group of entries concerned other profits from justice. Under the heading *Nova placita et novae conventiones* appeared all the sums levied by the itinerant justices on their eyres for the current year, knowledge of which was obtained from consulting the plea rolls of the justices. Immediately following came a section devoted to amercements levied for infraction against the royal forest. Finally, under the rubric *De catallis fugitivorum et mutilatorum* (concerning the chattels of fugitives and mutilated persons) were the amounts obtained from the sale of the possessions of criminals.

All just described comprised the account rendered by the sheriff for his county. For each county the arrangement was the same. In the twelfth century accounts were rendered for about thirty to thirty-three counties. The only sums not appearing in the sheriffs' accounts were those in accounts rendered separately by certain boroughs and honors. In the twelfth century there were about fourteen such boroughs. Lincoln, Winchester, and London, for example, had the privilege of rendering their own accounts; so, too, did a varying number of honors[1]. These accounts, though much smaller than those of the counties, followed the same arrangement. Generally the accounts of the boroughs and honors came at the end of the entries of the county in which they were located.

After the sheriff had accounted for all the items listed in and outside the farm of his county the final state of his account was

---

[1] The privilege of the boroughs to render their own accounts was known as the *firma burgi*. See C. Stephenson, *Borough and Town* (Cambridge, Mass., 1933), pp. 110-111, 166-170, and J. Tait, *The Mediaeval English Borough* (Manchester, 1936), pp. 139-193.

determined. Attention was now focussed upon the space after the words *In Thesauro*. Here the scribe entered the total amount paid into the exchequer. If the sheriff had satisfactorily accounted for all the debts, he was declared quit and the words *Et quietus est* were written in the space. If the sheriff still owed money, the amount would be entered after the words *Et debet* and would appear as arrears in the Pipe Roll of the following year. If the sheriff paid in more money than was due, the surplus sum would be entered after the phrase *Et habet de superplus* and would be credited to him the following year. The proper entries having been made, the figures indicating the total amount paid by the sheriff into the exchequer were written at the head of the account of his county. This entry was written last so as to avoid the risk of making an erasure. The sheriff had now settled his account until the following year and was free to return to his county and to his administrative tasks.

5. *Tentative Conclusions*

A concluding chapter will summarize the results of this study of financial institutions during the eleventh and twelfth centuries but at this point it will be helpful to clarify what have emerged as the principal similarities and contrasts in the financial systems of England and Flanders.

Much less a product of Carolingian government and tradition than that of Flanders, English government in the eleventh and twelfth centuries still resembled those continental institutions which looked back to a common Carolingian ancestor. No clear distinction can be made between large and small council, but in both Flanders and England the small council was in fact the chief governing organ which gave the ruler his most valuable counsel and implemented the decisions made. Here was the nerve center of medieval government; here was concentrated the talent which provided constant government and direction. In both Flanders and England the small council was intimately associated with the household whose officers such as the chancellor and chamberlains were key members of the small council and who early assumed control over finance. In Flanders and England where efficient financial institutions outpaced those of neighboring states, finance was centered in the household, that is the chamber, down to the late eleventh and early twelfth centuries. The chamber not only received, stored, and disbursed revenues in kind and in cash but also kept accounts and supervised the territorial officers who collected and occasionally disbursed revenues, some of which had already been lumped into a yearly set income or farm.

The late eleventh century was a period of important financial innovation in Flanders and England. To meet new financial demands imposed by the economic revival of western Europe and by expanding government, institutions had to be revamped and made less personal and domestic. In England quite some time before 1100 a treasury at Winchester had budded off from the chamber and, although staffed primarily by chamber personnel, had assumed and expanded functions previously those of the chamber. Unlike the chamber this treasury was not itinerant. From its Winchester base it received revenues from the sheriffs, stored and disbursed them, and kept the chamber supplied with adequate funds. And, moreover, this treasury accounted for the royal revenue and insured that the king received all that was due him in good coin. The Flemish reform of 1089 had a similar end. Although the chamber remained the principal treasury where revenues were received and disbursed, the more important financial functions such as supervision of territorial receivers and periodic accounting were placed in the hands of the chancellor and his assistants. As in England finance became more efficient, professional, and impersonal. As in England there were now financial circumscriptions headed by non-feudal officers, the *notarii*, who were accountable to a central organ of control known as the *redeninge*.

The English financial innovation under Henry I, which emerged in the form of the exchequer, went far beyond the Flemish reform of 1089 but its objective was the same—the centralization of finance in a group of men concerned primarily and almost daily with the supervision of the royal income. In almost every respect the English exchequer of the twelfth century was more advanced than the Flemish *redeninge*. The annual auditing sessions were better organized, the accountable officers more strictly supervised, the Pipe Rolls more detailed and accurate than the *Grote Brieven*, the system of reckoning accounts more sophisticated, and the conversion of incomes in kind to money more rapid. In the larger and more powerful English state such institutional advance is readily understandable; what needs reiteration is the fundamental likeness of exchequer and *redeninge*, of Pipe Roll and *Grote Brief*, of territorial administration, and of the financial lead enjoyed by Flanders and England over the rest of western Europe. Where, except possibly in Sicily and Normandy, could there be found in the twelfth century such intelligent financial administration? Where else could there be found such centralization, accurate records, the use of the abacus, and the efficient territorial organization?

England outpaced Flanders but the financial techniques and objectives were alike. This common institutional development is too striking to permit our viewing English institutions apart from those of Flanders or those of western Europe. *Au fond* there was a similar institutional response to common political, economic, and social forces.

CHAPTER V

SYNTHESIS

However diverse, the influence of Carolingian institutions upon those of the feudal Europe that emerged in the tenth and eleventh centuries must be recognized as a major force in the evolution of medieval institutions. Looking across eleventh-century Europe and into the governments characteristic of the feudal states, one sees everywhere the Carolingian heritage. Each feudal prince had a large court composed of intimate and less intimate members, most of whom were vassals. Though this large court helped the prince to govern and make his most important decisions, it was not in continuous session and therefore did not provide constant government. This was the function of the small court that did all and more than was done by the large court except helping to make major decisions or laws. This small court, comprising valued friends of the prince and men experienced in government, was the nerve center of government, responsible for what we would call administration.

Often difficult to distinguish from the small court was the household whose members, friends and competent functionaries very close to the prince, ministered to his physical, domestic, and official needs. The household not only worked closely with the small court but some of its personnel belonged to the small court and supervised such technical aspects of government as record-keeping and finance. Though with variations, such government was typically Carolingian and prevailed in continental states like Flanders, Normandy, and the French royal domain. Except for feudal principles and practices central government in Anglo-Saxon England was about the same. There is some evidence for the view of certain historians that Anglo-Saxon government was influenced by Carolingian institutions, but such influence could not have been strong until introduced in the form of Norman institutions after 1066. Despite the opportunities that existed between the ninth and eleventh centuries for the introduction of Carolingian principles of government, Anglo-Saxon government, it must be concluded, developed largely on its own. And yet, curiously, it must be recognized that Anglo-Saxon government by 1066 was little different from that of the continental states of Flanders, Normandy, and the French royal domain. Let us keep this similarity in mind as we come to some conclusions on the financial institutions of western Europe in the eleventh and twelfth centuries.

Prior to the eleventh century lack of pertinent sources, itself an indication of the miserable economic conditions, hinders the study of financial institutions in western Europe. References in charters and narrative sources suggest, however, a primitive system of finance centered in the princely households, specifically in the chamber, where valuables were traditionally kept and guarded. Until the eleventh century the chamber with a small staff of one or, at the most, three chamberlains assisted by a few clerks easily handled the private and public financial needs of the prince. There was no need for a large treasury and staff, written records, accounting, and an elaborate organization for the collection of revenue. During the eleventh century, however, the reviving economy changed this situation; the chamber expanded, reorganized its operations, and gave way to more efficient methods of financial administration.

Until almost 1066 financial administration in Anglo-Saxon England centered exclusively in the chamber staffed by a master chamberlain, two assistant chamberlains, and some minor functionaries. During the eleventh century the chamber had expanded its functions to receive the annual farms from the sheriffs of the shires as well as other extraordinary revenues. By 1066 most of the income was received in money and that still in kind was converted into money values. Accounting procedures had been established to check annually the sheriffs and other accountants. To insure the receipt of good money, methods had been devised to weigh and test the coins. Wooden tallies were given as receipts and served as vouchers. On the eve of the

Norman Conquest it had been necessary for the chamber to establish a second treasury at Winchester which, staffed by chamber personnel, stored and disbursed money and began to assume other chamber functions.

Though in organization the Anglo-Saxon chamber was more advanced than those across the Channel, there were striking similarities. Even in early eleventh-century Normandy under Duke Richard II there was a chamber which received and disbursed ducal revenue. Certain incomes were already fixed and anticipated the farms received later in the century from the *vicomtés* and *prévôtés*. Cash incomes were steadily superseding those in kind and, despite scanty evidence, it seems certain that records were kept of the receipts and disbursements. This chamber organization continued down to the reign of Henry I in the early twelfth century when most of the chamber's functions were then assumed by the exchequer.

In Flanders by the early twelfth century there was a chamber staffed by a master chamberlain, one or two assistant chamberlains, and a *notarius* who provided secretarial assistance. Incomes from the comital domain were collected and rendered by territorial receivers, some of whom were called *notarii*. Receipt of incomes in kind was more prevalent than in England but the trend was to substitute money and to convert incomes in kind into money values. That there was already a primitive accounting system which forced the territorial receivers to account yearly to the chamber for the revenues due seems likely.

Until the reign of Louis VII Capetian finance is enveloped in darkness and all that may be said is that there was a chamber in the eleventh century and that under Philip I (1060-1108) a *dispensator* looked after the financial needs of the king. Certainly revenues were received from local territorial circumscriptions but they seem to have been mostly in kind. In every respect Capetian financial administration lagged behind that of Normandy and Flanders and appears pathetic when compared to that of the Anglo-Saxon kings. Clearly the superior political strength and organization of Flanders, Normandy, and England are reflected in the level of financial administration. To speculate that this administrative lead was also connected with economic recovery and productivity seems justified, especially with reference to England and Normandy. It is surprising that in Flanders where at this time trade and industry clearly outpaced the rest of Europe so much of the comital revenue was still in kind. We may be unaware of money incomes available to the counts but the evidence forces us to conclude that institutional adjustment was not in tune with the Flemish economy.

Into the last half of the eleventh century the chamber was able to cope with princely finance, but at this point modifications of major proportions came. They came first in England and Flanders where expanding government, centralization, and economic growth forced greater efficiency in financial institutions. In England some time before 1066 it had been necessary to establish a treasury at Winchester to store increased revenues and to assist the chamber in the disbursement of money. In this treasury, which was but a sedentary branch of the chamber staffed by the parent organization, was sown the seed for the creation of a treasury that was soon to supersede the chamber as the center of royal finance. By the early twelfth century the treasury at Winchester had detached itself from the chamber and assumed most of its functions; finance had for the first time gone out of court and household. Because there was never a clear-cut distinction in the Middle Ages between private and public finance, the chamber continued its role in what would be regarded today as public finance, but this role, except for certain periods, was limited to the private or domestic needs of the kings. Henceforth the treasury received most of the revenue, supplied most of the chamber's money, audited accounts, tested the coins, and made most of the large disbursements. In the early part of Henry I's reign the treasury was in effect a pre-exchequer.

The Flemish financial reform of 1089, though not as extensive as the English, had some similar objectives. The chamber retained its position as the place where revenues were received and disbursed and the chamberlain and his assistants remained the principal staff. Finance stayed in the household. What changed was the element of control. Henceforth the domanial revenues of the counts were subjected to annual audits placed under the control of the chancellor who, though a member of the household and court, was not daily concerned with finance. Under his supervision the accounts of all the territorial receivers were audited. Over both chamber and local financial officers there was now an outside control that was soon to demand an increased supervision of the comital court and a more sophisticated system of record-keeping and testing of money.

In the early twelfth century English and Flemish financial organization was ahead of that in Normandy and the French royal domain. Lacking evidence we can but suggest that political turbulence in Normandy under Robert Curthose and in the royal domain under Philip I and Louis VI blocked institutional advance. Only when peace came to Normandy after the victory of Henry I at Tinchebrai in 1106 could administration improve. It soon did, and then the traditional chamber organization was replaced by the Norman exchequer. Although Louis VI laid the foundation for orderly institutional development in the royal domain, only with the reign of Philip Augustus was the king powerful enough politically and economically to make progress in financial administration. Until the early thirteenth century there are no financial records; throughout most of the twelfth century it must be assumed that the royal chamber remained in control of the revenues coming from the *prévôtés*.

The late eleventh and early twelfth centuries formed a transitional period wherein princely finance was compelled by new economic and political demands to expand and to become less domestic. Working with the chamber but independent and having assumed a paramount position in finance was the English treasury. In Flanders the chancellor was given control over the accounts of the territorial receivers, which indirectly gave him control over the chamber. Normandy was on the verge of financial reorganization. Only in the French royal domain was there no change. From such transition arose innovations that were to determine the course of financial institutions for the rest of the Middle Ages.

In many respects the English treasury of the early twelfth century resembled its successor, the exchequer, which began functioning about the middle of Henry I's reign. That part of the exchequer known as the Lower Exchequer served as a storehouse for money and took over the functions of the treasury. The Upper Exchequer was where the changes occurred. When the members of the royal court who composed the Upper Exchequer met semi-annually to audit the accounts they were in reality the small court sitting in a financial capacity, and when they adjudicated financial cases, also in a judicial capacity. Only the treasurer and his assistants were primarily concerned with the operations of the exchequer; when the auditing was completed the other members went on to other work of the royal court. Innovation came with the introduction of curial control and accurate written records in the form of the Pipe Rolls. Use of the abacus to improve reckoning of the accounts and refinement of methods for testing the coins aided this control. The exchequer remained the principal financial department for the rest of the Middle Ages. With its own personnel and tradition it functioned daily as treasury and office of records; augmented twice a year by members of the small court it became an auditing and judicial body. Though as much a royal organ as the old treasury and chamber, the exchequer was sedentary and not so close to the king. Its principal concern was public finance. The chamber, relegated mostly to managing the private finances of the king, continued to receive some money directly from royal debtors but most of its supply came from the exchequer to which it became accountable. There were now three financial bodies —the Upper Exchequer (an auditing body), the Lower Exchequer (treasury), and the chamber. The three cooperated to provide amazingly efficient financial administration for the Norman-Angevin kings.

Less well informed about the Norman exchequer, we can nevertheless find its development during the reign of Henry I. As in England it then superseded the chamber as the primary financial organization and so remained until the loss of Normandy to Philip Augustus in 1204. Henceforth the treasury of the exchequer at Caen (the counterpart of the English Lower Exchequer) received the traditional revenues previously owed to the chamber by the *vicomtés* and *prévôtés*. Semi-annually, at Easter and Michaelmas, the accounts of the territorial receivers

were audited by barons of the exchequer who, like their counterparts in England, comprised the royal court sitting in a financial
capacity. Like the English exchequer the Norman was also a
court of law. When not concerned with auditing or adjudicating
financial cases the members of the court concentrated on other
business of the duchy. As in England the money was received,
tested, stored, and disbursed; and records were kept of the
transactions. Besides the chief treasury at Caen lesser ones were
strategically located throughout the duchy. As early as the reign
of Henry I the principles of the abacus had been applied to
the auditing of accounts. It is still debatable whether the abacus
was used first in Normandy or England and where the exchequer
first arose. What can be said is that the English evidence ante-
dates the Norman by a few years. More essential is to stress
that the Norman and English exchequers evolved at the same
time, had the same basic features, and kept the same type of
record. Each had its own permanent staff, augmented at the
auditing sessions by barons of the exchequer comprised of men
who represented both the Norman and English sides of the
royal court. There was regular communication between the
exchequers, information was exchanged, sums and personnel
were transferred. Both worked for the same strict Norman-
Angevin masters.

The historian studying financial institutions in Flanders faces
the same obstacle that exists for Normandy—lack of adequate
sources until the last quarter of the twelfth century. As in
Normandy it is certain that innovation in central financial organization pre-dated the records. Years prior to the *Grote Brief* of
1187 Flemish finance had advanced beyond the reform of 1089.
As in England and Normandy renovation took finance farther
out of the household and attempted to create closer liaison
between central and territorial administration. It is possible that
by the late eleventh century there was an annual auditing session
of territorial accounts held in June. The chancellor, representing
the count and the comital court, was in charge of the session
attended by the receivers of some forty circumscriptions. What
probably occurred in the twelfth century, though it cannot be
documented, is that other members of the court joined the

chancellor in a supervisory capacity. On such an occasion the comital court sat in a financial capacity and did what was done by the barons of the Norman and English exchequers. Just as the Norman-Angevin kings could and occasionally did preside over the exchequer sessions, so could and did the Flemish counts over the *redeninge*. Normally, however, these sessions were presided over by the chancellor just as they were by the justiciar in England and the seneschal in Normandy. Whatever the date of introduction, the principles of the abacus were applied to the accounting, as they were likewise to the regional accounting sessions which may have anticipated the annual *redeninge* for the whole of Flanders and which were undoubtedly preliminary auditings preparatory to the final accounting. Assays of coins like those in England and Normandy were standard procedure. And records not unlike the Norman and English Pipe Rolls recorded the transactions.

What differed most was the role of the treasury in central administration. In England it was the treasury which had broken off from the chamber and had assumed the principal financial functions, and which was incorporated into the exchequer under Henry I. In Normandy the *camera* was the *thesaurus* and handled intimate ducal as well as territorial finance until superseded by the exchequer under Henry I when the treasury functions of the chamber were lost and the chamber (the same part of the household whether the king was in England or Normandy) was essentially relegated to privy finance. In Flanders the evolution was different. As in Normandy the *camera* was the *thesaurus*, but the latter did not split off from the former with the reform of 1089, and no real separation occurred even later in the twelfth century when exchequer-like procedure in the form of the *redeninge* became regularized. While English and Norman finance became tripartite, Flemish became only bipartite. In Flanders, smaller than either Normandy or England and so much smaller than the Norman-Angevin territory in the twelfth century, there was no need to create a treasury apart from that of the household. The comital money was placed in storage depots of the chamber but was never put under a separate personnel. In reality the *notarius* of the late twelfth century who headed a *thesaurus* was but a servant of an *appanage* of the chamber. Even later in the thirteenth century when new incomes as well as the financial operations of the *hôtel* were placed under the control of a commission composed of members of the comital court, the division of labor did not radically change.

While basic financial reform came to England, Normandy, and Flanders in the twelfth century, it was not so with the French royal domain. This lag, though explicable in terms of political and economic retardation, is surprising in contrast with the administrative advance made under Philip Augustus in the early thirteenth century. Certainly it was only in the reign of Philip Augustus that there were the political strength and economic resources essential for any well-organized financial administration. With the conquest of Normandy and other Angevin possessions in the early thirteenth century much of the Angevin administration became the model for Capetian. And with the catastrophe of Count Ferrand at Bouvines in 1214 subsequent French intervention in Flemish politics and the annexation of Flemish territory gave the Capetians still more institutional knowledge. These events coincide with Capetian institutional advance in the thirteenth century. What evidence exists, however, points to some reorganization of finance even before the change in Capetian political fortunes, probably as early as the reign of Louis VII. By 1146 there obviously was need of a larger and more sedentary treasury than provided by the chamber, because at this time the financial organization of the Knights Templars came to be used; the treasury was placed in the Temple and staffed by the Templars. Here was stored the royal money and from here came the chamber's supply. Under Philip Augustus reorganization of territorial administration and attempts at tighter control seem to be connected with the beginning of accounts of expenses of the *bailliages* and *prévôtés* audited by a central body. Such auditing must have begun under Philip Augustus because the general financial account of 1202-1203 is a record of the accounts of the *bailliages* and *prévôtés* audited by a part of the royal court, the so-called *curia in compotis*, acting in a financial capacity. Only with Philip Augustus did Capetian administration begin to approximate that long established in the neighboring states. Then the auditing body of the royal court *(curia in compotis)* compared to the auditing parts of the Norman and English exchequers and to the Flemish *redeninge*. While the Temple, literally a bank used by the Capetians, was the treasury, it had no permanent royal staff or close attachment to the organ of control. To it went the royal income and from it came the disbursements. The chamber restricted itself largely to privy finance and drew its funds from the Temple. By the early thirteenth century, however, French financial administration had not overtaken that in the other three states and would not until the reign of Saint Louis.

The cruel losses of medieval financial records on the Continent does not alone explain the richer English documentation. From what is known about English financial organization between the early eleventh and the thirteenth centuries it is apparent that the earlier and more numerous records reflect a more advanced institutional development. But having made this observation, one must note that English administration did not far outpace that of Normandy and Flanders. Though records such as the *Grote Brief* and the Norman Pipe Rolls are extant only with the last quarter of the twelfth century, fragments of auxiliary records indicate an institutional advance not much behind that of England. Without doubt, however, the lack of records for the eleventh and twelfth centuries in the French royal domain suggests more than subsequent loss of records as the explanation. Not until Philip Augustus was there the administration that could produce such records.

In basic information the general financial accounts of the four states were alike; they differed only in such details as the order of the fiscal circumscriptions in the accounts, particular type of incomes and disbursements, and local peculiarities. The Norman and English Pipe Rolls rested upon the same system of accounting, and that of the Flemish *Grote Brief* was somewhat similar. The English and Norman Pipe Rolls, being for larger areas, were more bulky. The composition of all the accounts was much the same; most of the information was known prior to the redaction of the final account and was placed, even before the final auditing session, on the account or upon preliminary records whose contents were incorporated into the final general account. In all four states the general accounts symbolize the rulers' control via their courts over finance and demonstrate a tight surveillance over financial institutions, either central or local.

Local organization was more varied. In England the shire from the middle of the tenth century had been a financial district for which the sheriff was responsible and for which he remained responsible under the Norman and Angevin kings. Assisted by subordinates, such as the officers who administered the hundreds and royal manors, the sheriff was the officer solely responsible for the revenues from his shire and for the disbursements made from those revenues; he was accountable to a central auditing board, be it the chamber, treasury, or exchequer. Never was he a feudal officer, either before or after the Norman Conquest; he received royal remuneration and was appointed or dismissed by the king. Seldom, despite his enormous power which extended to every aspect of local shire administration, did the sheriff challenge the royal authority. Each sheriff was subjected to strict control and each nervously faced the ordeal of the semi-annual auditing sessions in the Upper Exchequer. In Normandy the *vicomtes* and *prévôts* were the officers responsible for financial administration in the *vicomtés* and *prévôtés* and had been so at least since the rule of William the Conqueror. Like the sheriffs they were responsible for all local government and were assisted by subordinates. They, too, were the sole officers accountable to the Norman exchequer. Unlike the sheriffs, however, they held their offices in fief and posed more of a challenge to princely authority. After Henry I placed Normandy under royal rule, control was tightened and became about as effective as in England. Only later, especially when Normandy passed under Capetian rule, were these feudal officers replaced by the non-feudal bailiffs.

The situation in the French royal domain resembled that in Normandy. Until the late twelfth century the *prévôts* were the officers accountable for the incomes of the *prévôtés* to the *curia in compotis*. They, too, were feudal officers and only disappeared when Philip Augustus began replacing the old feudal adminis-

trators with non-feudal bailiffs. At this point the financial functions of the *prévôts* were farmed out to other officials and, as
the *prévôtés* were organized into *bailliages*, the functions of the
bailiffs were extended to the collection of extraordinary and
casual incomes not connected with the old domanial incomes.

In Flanders local finance was more complicated. During the
eleventh and twelfth centuries the *châtelains*, who were comparable to the English sheriffs and the Norman and Capetian
vicomtes and *prévôts*, had no financial duties, but, as feudal
officers, had principally military and judicial functions. Local
financial officers, whose fiscal circumscriptions, sometimes coter-
minous with a *châtellenie* but more often smaller, comprised but
one of several financial districts *(officia)* of a *châtellenie*, were
accountable to the chancellor and the *redeninge*. Occasionally
some local *prepositus* or *preco* would render account directly to
the chancellor but usually this was the responsibility of the
notarii who were the fiscal heads of the *officia* in the late eleventh
and twelfth centuries. There were local and subordinate officers
under the *notarii* who collected revenues and rendered account
to them. The non-feudal *notarii* were in some respects like the
English sheriffs who were solely responsible for rendering accounts to a central auditing body, but while the sheriffs combined
the functions of *notarii* and *châtelains*, the *notarii* were limited
to strictly financial duties.

During the second half of the twelfth century local Flemish
financial administration seemed to retrogress when the non-
feudal *notarii* were replaced by noble laymen, the *redenaars*, who
were feudal officers. Perhaps, as Professor Verhulst has suggested, the change from non-feudal to feudal administration was
not as crucial as it might seem because the old domanial revenues
administered by the *redenaars* became less important while the
new and more lucrative extraordinary and non-domanial revenues came to be collected by special receivers accountable under
a new administrative arrangement to the chamberlain. The other
successors to the duties of the *notarii* were the bailiffs who
appeared in the last quarter of the twelfth century. These new
officers, with judicial and financial functions, were non-feudal
and resembled the English sheriff and the bailiffs of Normandy

and the French royal domain. Though chiefly concerned with justice and the collection of the profits of justice, bailiffs collected certain domanial revenues and assumed responsibility for some casual expenses of the counts. On balance, therefore, the Flemish trend in administration was, as in the other states, towards defeudalization of key officers. Appearing earlier perhaps than his counterpart in Normandy and the French royal domain, the Flemish bailiff certainly stimulated the transition from feudal to non-feudal administration.

The types of income received by the rulers of the four states varied but slightly. The incomes came from the princely domains and from such revenues as tolls and extraordinary taxes not derived from the old seignorial economy. Excluding the French royal domain because the records are insufficient, we know that during the twelfth century in England, Normandy, and Flanders the domanial revenues steadily declined while the new non-domanial revenues increased. This trend reflects the marked shift from an agrarian to a money economy, a situation seen also by the replacement of incomes in kind with those in money. Although in Flanders the incomes in kind were all converted into money values, at the end of the twelfth century the counts of Flanders still received a considerable portion of their revenues in kind. This was also true for the French royal domain where in the early thirteenth century disbursements in kind were still common, more so than in Flanders. In England and Normandy, however, all incomes were received in money. Economic retardation can explain why incomes and payments in kind lingered on in the royal domain but other reasons must be sought for Flanders, which in the twelfth century was economically ahead of England and Normandy. Perhaps incomes in kind clung on longer in Flanders because administration was slightly less progressive. Conversion probably could have come more rapidly but did not, because slower administrative change meant that traditional financial practices were less abruptly challenged and transformed. One's overall impression at the beginning of the thirteenth century, even in the French royal domain, is of a marked shrinkage in value of traditional agrarian incomes and of the rise of revenues from new monetary sources.

If the expenses of the English rulers exceeded those of their contemporaries in Flanders and the French royal domain, this was the only significant difference. All the rulers had the same expenses to meet and all had broken them down into fixed-annual expenses and those of a casual and fluctuating value. These expenses were handled in two ways. Either the territorial receivers made payments out of the revenues collected directly and were credited for the payments, or debtors were paid from the central treasury. Tradition and convenience generally dictated which system was used. When, for example, a monastery received an annual fixed sum, the payment was usually made from the revenues of the circumscription in which the monastery was located. The salaries and expenses of local administration were similarly met. When princely financial obligations were not localized then it was more practical to pay them from the central treasury.

Common to the financial administration of the four states was the farm system first found in England as early as the Anglo-Saxon period. Incomes from shires were partially farmed before Edward the Confessor and by his reign it is possible that all the incomes from some shires were farmed by the sheriffs. Probably set sums had already been calculated as the farms of the shires due annually. After 1066 this system was extended to all the shires and all the incomes received at the treasury were in money. In Normandy the farm system was certainly known before 1066 and was subsequently generalized to the point where all *vicomtés* and *prévôtés* owed round sums rendered in cash. The Norman system was basically like the English except that it developed more slowly and that the conversion from kind to money was more gradual. Not until the reign of Henry I was the farm system as generalized and as well administered as in England.

Even at the end of the twelfth century not all the fiscal circumscriptions of Flanders were farmed. Some were completely farmed and some but partially. In circumscriptions where incomes were farmed, one notes a transition to money payments, but farms still continued to be rendered in kind. One cannot say much about the farm system in the French royal domain until the thirteenth century. Then the account of 1202-1203 shows a farm system generalized to include all the *prévôtés*, with each owing a lump cash sum yearly. This farm system was more efficient than that of Flanders and less complicated than that of Normandy. Perhaps Philip Augustus observed both the Norman and Flemish systems, discarded the less efficient aspects, and adopted those practices that appeared most useful. So little had royal finance been organized prior to his reign it must have been relatively simple to innovate. Old practices and traditions were not the obstacles that they were in Flanders and Normandy.

Any historian would like to know the conversation of medieval princes and that of their advisers and functionaries. Did they compare notes and did they attempt to learn from each other? This question the records do not satisfactorily answer. Certainly in the corner of western Europe we have chosen to study, proximity and frequent contact facilitated the exchange of information and observation of other administrative systems. That this occurred for England and Normandy after 1066 is apparent. Although English finance was ahead of Norman in most respects, both systems borrowed procedures and learned from the other. A common master and common officials facilitated this interplay. On the other hand it must be acknowledged that comparable financial systems had evolved in England and Normandy prior to 1066 when borrowing could not have been of much importance.

It is evident that, except for details explained by local custom and need and except for chronological variation in institutional development caused by regional political and economic conditions, the financial systems of Flanders, the French royal domain, and Normandy were essentially alike. We have admitted that the Carolingian heritage was definitely a molding force which gave common characteristics to continental institutions, and that the high degree of feudalization in western Europe was also such a force. But more than common heritage and institutional borrowing produced these common features. Degree of political power, economic resources, and local need, whether in England or on the Continent, governed what rulers and their administrators did or could do with their institutions. These ingredients more than heritage and borrowing account for the common characteristics of the financial institutions of western Europe during their formative period in the eleventh and twelfth centuries. This common bond between institutions, not as visible perhaps as that which united the church of western Christendom or that which gave thought and art a like vocabulary and expression, nevertheless existed. And its existence suggests that the study of institutions, traditionally so local and so particularistic, should be abandoned for the more meaningful comparative approach. Just as it is more interesting and significant to know the features of scholastic thought, Gothic architecture, and ecclesiastical organization common to western Europe rather than to dwell solely on their local differences, so it is with medieval institutions. From the elements it holds in common has the civilization of western Europe flourished and will it continue to flourish.

INDEX

abacus, 39–40, 67–68, 71, 87–89
Adelard of Bath, 67
aid, 78
Aire, 24
amercements, 78
Anglo-Saxon government, 82–83
Arnold, chamberlain of Flanders, 13–15

bailiffs, 18, 26–27, 45, 93–94
bailliages, 44–47, 90, 93
Baldwin IX, count of Flanders, charter of, 33
balfart, 75
Bapaume, 21, 25, 31–32
Basilius, *notarius*, 16
boroughs, 78
Borrelli de Serres, 46
Bouvines, 90; battle of, 11
brevia, 18–21, 25–27, 31, 34–35, 39, 45–46, 67, 73
brevia camere, 18
brevia et annotationes, 17
breviatores, 14
Bruges, 12, 14, 18, 20, 24, 39–40, 49, 56–57, 61
burthegn, 56

caisse de la cour, 42
calculator, 69
camera, 15–16, 19, 37, 42, 56–57, 89
camerarii, 42, 56
camera-thesaurus, 41
caput, 29–30, 35–36, 73
Carolingian government, 53–54, 79
Carolingian institutions, 82
Cassel, 24
castellani, 24
castellatura, 24
castra, 20
census, 31, 34

chamber, 57–58, 60–62, 69, 80, 83–85, 87, 89–91
chamberlain, 14–19, 54–56, 58, 61–63, 65, 69–70, 79, 83
chancellor, 54–55, 61–62, 65–66, 70, 79, 86, 88–89
Charles the Good, count of Flanders, 13, 15–16, 21
châtelains, 20–22, 25, 61, 93
châtellenies, 18, 20–21, 24–25, 61, 93
clerici, 25–26
county, 72, 78
Courtrai, 24, 34
curia, 28–29, 41–42, 66
curia comitis, 53
curia ducis, 53
curia in compotis, 42, 90–92
curia regis, 53, 70–71
curtes, 30–31

Danegeld, 59, 78
dapifer, 23–25
Delisle, L., 46
Dialogus de Scaccario, 71, 76
Diksmuide, 24, 30, 35
dispensatores, 21–26, 84
Domesday Book, 63
donum, 78

Exchequer: barons of, 70, 88; English, 9–10, 40, 59, 68–69, 76–77, 79–80, 86–88, 91; High Court of, 70; Lower, 70–71, 87; Norman, 9–10, 48, 87–88, 91–92; Upper, 70–71, 87, 92
expenses: casual, 95; fixed, 75, 95; occasional, 75

farm, 32–33, 35, 48–52, 58–59, 76–78, 83, 95–96
fiefs-rentes, 75

98

BARON FRIEDRICH VON HÜGEL
AND THE MODERNIST CRISIS IN ENGLAND